mechanical fa

The Homoerotic Journal (
with Illustrations by Gwe

Patrick J Cowle

In Memory of Patrick Joseph Cowley
(October, 19 1950 - November, 12 1982)

First Edition 2019

ISBN: 978-1-942884-54-5

Text design by Wolfgang Schneider

Cover design and all artwork by Gwenaël Rattke

Editing by Jorge Socarrás and Josh Cheon

The text for this book is set in Korinna

Printed in Germany by Druckhaus Berlin-Mitte

DARK ENTRIES EDITIONS,
835 Larkin St, San Francisco, CA 94109
www.darkentriesrecords.com

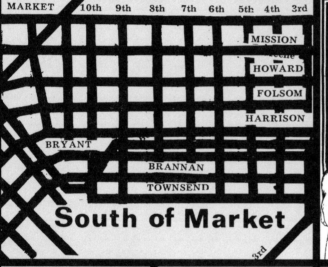

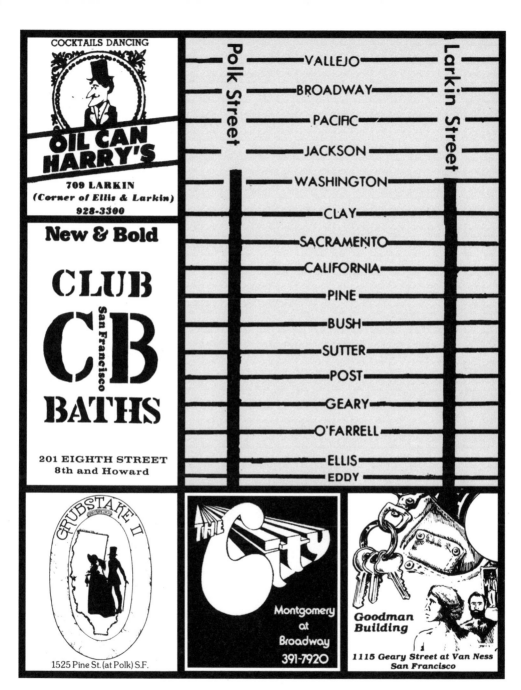

Timelink BY JOSH CHEON

Patrick Cowley came into my life in June 2006 through a lover who played me *Mind Warp* as he rolled a joint on the LP jacket. A month later, I visited San Francisco for the first time, fell in love and moved west. The following year I joined Honey Soundsystem, a crew of gay discaires. In November 2007 John Hedges, former co-owner of Megatone Records with Patrick, bequeathed his record collection, including three boxes of reel-to-reel tapes, to us before retiring to Palm Springs. In June 2008 Honey hosted a party with Stefan Goldmann and we gave him two CD-Rs with digital transfers of the tapes. Stefan was crazy about the "Catholic" project Patrick recorded with Jorge Socarrás and released it on his label MACRO. To celebrate, Honey organized a record release party in SF on October 19, 2009, Patrick's 59th birthday. I decided to track down as many of Patrick's friends as I could and interview them. At the release party Chris Njirich, of Hi-NRG group BearEssence, asked if I had found Patrick's gay porn soundtracks. Bewildered, I did some sleuthing and discovered Patrick credited on 3 films by Fox Studio. I tracked down director John Coletti, who was living in LA and flew down for a meeting. In the Fox Studio archives I unearthed 8 reels of Patrick's music. Over the next few years all 3 soundtracks would be released on my label Dark Entries: *School Daze* (2013), *Muscle Up* (2015) and *Afternooners* (2017). In September 2017 I asked Patrick's former roommate Theresa McGinley to perform at the *Afternooners* record release party. She asked to read from Patrick's sex journal. "WHAT? YES!" I said flabbergasted and knew we had to publish it unedited, though some typos have been silently corrected. We've included Patrick's doodles too. As Patrick's muse Candida Royalle told me in 2009, "It has dawned on me, that we only live as long as we're remembered. With someone like Patrick who leaves this wonderful body of innovative music, he's gonna live a long time and that is wonderful and so deserving, and I'm so grateful for that."

Foreword BY THERESA McGINLEY

When I met Patrick Cowley he was a virgin and so was I. It was my good fortune to meet him in 1968 when we were both still teenagers. We talked a great deal about sex, a subject that fell into the realm of sacred mysteries. Along with sex, we discussed music, literature, poetry, films, and the struggle to throw off the yoke of our conservative Roman Catholic upbringings. As college students we espoused anti-establishment sentiments and participated in Vietnam War protests. We were not supposed to hang on to our virtue, so said the zeitgeist. Eventually, we both lost our virginities, separately.

Several months after the Stonewall riots, and after I indicated to Patrick that I was questioning my own sexuality, Patrick came out. First he confided only to me that he was homosexual. Up until then, he had never had sex with a man. It was not easy for him to come out to our circle of friends, much less to his family, but Patrick knew what he wanted to do. Shortly after that confession he moved to San Francisco.

In 1971 Patrick gave me the gift of a plane ticket to join him in San Francisco. He was ebullient when he met me at the airport, and declared that he had found his people and wanted to share this new world. We moved into a tiny apartment that faced the Panhandle on Oak Street in the Haight-Ashbury. Together, we delighted in joining the counterculture and discovering what we saw as visionary perspectives. Along with participating in the exciting *mise en scène,* Patrick pursued his creative interests, with emphasis on music.

When Patrick was ill in the early '80s, I helped with caretaking and eventually moved into a flat in his Castro neighborhood home. He was one of the early AIDS victims who did not stand a chance against the virus. As his body weakened, his emotions grew stronger. We talked less about sex, and more about feelings. He did not lament his choices, but he divulged his regret that he hadn't kept a long-term lover. Had he been given more time, I am certain he would have grown to be the loving partner of a fortunate man.

There are those readers who might flinch at Patrick's record of his sexual escapades. In fact, he feared his family would do just that and destroy his sex journal if it were to be found after he had died. Therefore, he asked me to keep it for him and to save it from the scrap heap, as he put it. I carried the unread journal with me for many years.

In 2009, around the same time that new interest in Patrick's work was developing, Josh Cheon came upon some of Patrick's unpublished tapes that had been languishing in an attic for years. After Josh digitized many of the recordings, new facets of Patrick's musical explorations were uncovered and enthusiasm for his work expanded. Samples of much more than the Hi-NRG dance music Patrick had recorded in his lifetime were reissued, including his pre-disco collaborations with our mutual friends, Jorge Socarrás and Candice Vadala (aka Candida Royalle). At that juncture, I considered reading the journal. My sense of mortality was heightened a short time later when Candice was diagnosed with late-stage cancer. Consequently, I invited Jorge to read the journal with me. He and I honored our mutual friend on what would have been his 60th birthday by perusing the journal as we sat outdoors on one of the once-notorious piers in Lower Manhattan that Patrick mentions. We may not have read every word, but we touched every page.

Sexual disclosures are not for the faint of heart. Patrick was more than the product of a particular time and place. The sexual revolution and gay liberation movement catapulted his creativity. Both social and cultural platforms provided Patrick, a young Catholic man, the freedom to spurn dogmatic social conventions and be openly homosexual. Creating narratives with sound, rhythm, words, and composition is how Patrick transubstantiated his personal erotic experiences and fantasies into a Hi-NRG soundtrack for the club culture of the '70s and '80s. The amyl-fueled crowds sweating on dance floors made his influence on culture incarnate. This was part of the musical score of the era. His journal is not only a personal record but also a historic manuscript chronicling a milieu that was obliterated by the social upheaval caused by the AIDS epidemic.

The San Francisco gay community has not honored Patrick with a plaque on the Rainbow Honor Walk on Castro Street. Yet, this journal, along with his music, document Patrick Cowley's undeniable contribution to queer history. As Jorge Socarrás puts it, "Patrick is honored whenever people play, listen and dance to his music."

It is difficult to condense into a page or two the impact Patrick's friendship had on my life personally. He was the first individual I met who encouraged my creativity and I credit our friendship with inspiring me to explore it.

He may not have been the front man, but he definitely was a leading man and a Niagara of creativity.

Introduction BY JORGE SOCARRÁS

When Patrick Cowley and I started making music together in mid-1970s San Francisco, we went through a couple of names for our duo—"Good, Clean Fun" and "Lesserman"—before settling on "Catholic." Because we fancied ourselves wayward Catholic boys, it seemed perfectly succinct and ironic. It would be decades before I'd come to see how differently the Catholic imprint had manifested in each of us.

Ten years ago, Patrick's music, including our "Catholic" recordings, started resurfacing in unexpected ways. Around this time, his and my dear friend, Theresa McGinley, informed me that before dying he had given her his journal for safekeeping. Safekeeping because it was in fact a sex journal, which no doubt he wished to conserve from his less ironically Catholic family. Any prescience on his part beyond that prudent decision we can only speculate upon. In any case, Theresa had managed to stash the journal away all those years, and having refrained from reading it, finally decided that it was high time we do so—together. Patrick's ghost already newly influencing my life, the journal was another manifestation of what had until now been a primarily musical haunting.

As it turned out, Theresa decided she was passing the journal on to me, not only so that I could read it, but also because she thought I would know best what should be done with it. She felt that Patrick would have been in accord, and myself not having been there when he died, Theresa's intuition was my closest proximity. She and Patrick, presumably, were right: I knew immediately what should be done with the journal. What I didn't foresee were the new depths from which Patrick would haunt me.

That reading the journal should have shocked me was itself a kind of shock. Hardly a moralist, nor a stranger to Patrick's ways, I was his peer, collaborator, friend, at times more. Still, I had to read the journal in short intervals because I found it so very intense. It wasn't the details of his exploits; it was the sheer profusion, the obsessiveness and relentlessness. Not that Patrick ever hid his adventures from me; on the contrary, he relished recounting them. We shared our amorous and erotic tales much the way we shared music. I'd simply underestimated how fervent he was in his pursuits. Of course, bound together without interruption, when in reality there are often days between entries, heightens the effect considerably—and it *was* San Francisco in the '70s. Nonetheless Patrick's sexual insatiability stunned me in a deeply personal way. It made me see my own promiscuity at that time as relatively hippyish, contingent on the promise of free love that had lured me to San Francisco, as well as liberation from a Catholic upbringing. Patrick's sexual adventurousness was of another caliber—a fetishizing and mythologizing of the Catholic psyche, a reverse sublimation of religious impulse into erotic ritual.

Patrick had been the one who first declared we should make music together, so I was not entirely surprised when one day he audaciously pronounced, "I got you a membership card to the Jaguar Bookstore and you're coming with me." I knew that the backroom at the Jaguar Bookstore was a favorite setting of his sex life, and although I regularly passed by the storefront and was curious, I had never ventured in. After all, I could pick up guys right on Castro Street without a membership card. I had no qualm about having sex on a nude beach with a hippy friend of Patrick's in broad daylight, but I was still a virgin to backroom or bathhouse sex. Our collaborating on music having indeed proven such "good, clean, fun," I hardly questioned his determination to initiate me into this new sphere. However daunted or nervous I might have felt, he was excited and compelling enough for both of us. We smoked a joint, and before I knew it we were marching the couple of blocks from his house to Castro and 18th Street. Once in the bookstore, we flashed our cards at the desk clerk as if it were the library, and were buzzed through the members' door beyond the counter.

While I can't do a proper job of describing that backroom in much detail beyond the red filter of memory, I can assuredly say that it was stepping into another realm. I know that what happened happened; yet it was entirely removed from the everyday world—like walking onto a film set where everyone knew the scene and their parts. No matter that I didn't, because I was guided by more experienced players, each one's moves so ritualized that I fell right into the trancelike rhythm of it all. This was sex unlike any I'd experienced before, decidedly impersonal, an ancient rite through which bodies became vessels for the archetypal: the deity, the sacrifice, the priest and his attendants. Removed from time as it felt, the entire rite likely lasted no more than an hour. After I came back down to earth I saw Patrick standing at viewing distance, beaming, the proud progenitor of my initiation. He had evidently watched and savored it all as if the other men and I had indeed been actors in his own private erotic theater, his "mechanical fantasy box" as he might call it. What's more, he knew now that I understood, that the esoteric knowledge had been imparted.

As further confirmation of this mythic caliber of sexual experience, Patrick also took me to see my first gay porn film in a cinema. This was none other than Wakefield Poole's *Bijou*, its glittering, hallucinatory atmosphere forever conflated with my memory of the Jaguar backroom so that I cannot recall which came first, the actors in both equally archetypal, moving with the same choreographic deliberation. This then is how I came to understand Patrick's erotic sensibility, the ritualized religiosity he so ardently expresses throughout his journal, and his impelling drive to merge in divine consummation. Along with bodies, set, and lighting (another technical aspect in which Patrick achieved expertise), music was a key element in effecting that charged otherworldliness, and the synthesizer was the perfect instrument. On top of all the other music he was making, he started composing gay porn soundtracks as if they were accompaniment to his own fabulous fantasies. In effect they were. His journal lovingly documents those fantasies, fantasies that he acted out with a passionate intensity way beyond anything I had imagined. Reading it I came to see that my hour in the Jaguar was often his day-to-day. I shouldn't have been surprised that he was as tireless in his libidinal pursuits as he was in his musical endeavors, but I was blown away. I couldn't fathom how many sexual adventures he lived in the relatively brief intervals when we didn't see each other, nor how deeply into that other realm he probed. If I was an initiate, he was a high priest.

As the journal confirms, Patrick continued living his sexual fantasies with insatiable fervor for several years, seeking that quasi-religious high, trying anything with anyone who held the promise of orgasmic redemption, or at times an idealized romantic fulfillment. It's not until he started achieving greater musical success that he relented somewhat, and his self-reflections grow headier. He never mentions my initiation, and I don't know that he should have. He does however express his apprehension at my own obsession with shooting up speedballs, and that gave me pause. Was my fascination with needles my own sublimated Catholic ritual? Though Patrick never judged me, reading his entries it's evident how unwholesome he thought my injecting drugs. In an ironic twist, his darkest sexual exploits seem life-affirming compared to my own bloody proclivity. Through his eyes I have shocked myself.

Perhaps it's egoism, but there are moments when I can't help but speculate if Patrick might not have foreseen I'd one day read his journal. Nothing is too crazy once you cross over into the mythological. Thus it shouldn't seem strange that Theresa played Sibyl in facilitating the journal's destiny. No sooner had I started reading it than I knew it should be published. Also that it should have illustrations. The right artist would be able to further conjure that mythological world Patrick had reign to—not so much in concrete detail as in evocative fantasy. I also knew that this was a venture I wanted to realize together with Josh Cheon. My friendship with Josh had itself originated with the rediscovery of the "Catholic" music tapes that had been sequestered for some thirty years. Indeed the first photo of Josh and me together shows us smiling happily in front of a huge blowup photo of Patrick at the "Catholic" album release party in San Francisco. Having since come to know Josh's assiduous dedication to Patrick's musical legacy, there was no one better qualified to help expand that legacy into literary territory. Josh jumped right on board and everything started clicking into place. He suggested an artist with whom he had worked, Gwenaël Rattke, who had also done illustrating for a book about another remarkable person I had known, Cookie Mueller. We sent him a couple of journal excerpts to play with, and when we saw what he came up with, at once recognized that he was perfect for the project. Gwenaël dove into illustrating the journal with his own trancelike fervor, and the results would surely make Patrick grin with delight.

Patrick's journal is a testament to the zeitgeist of gay sexual liberation that shaped San Francisco in the 1970s. His music proved pivotal in fueling that extraordinary moment, the explosive gay sex scene that he thrived on, both on the dancefloor and in the backrooms. ("The boys in the backroom, laughing it up, shooting up menergy") In turn, the energy of that scene fueled his fantasies, and his fantasies inspired more music in a fiery wheel of reciprocal creation. I witnessed that energy in all its glory the night Patrick took me to Trocadero Transfer for the club debut of his Morodor/Donna Summer "I Feel Love" remix. All those hundreds of sexy men dancing, mostly shirtless, throwing their arms up in the air in blissful abandon, pumping up the menergy—I'd not seen anything like it. Thirty years later I saw that exalted scene spontaneously reenacted by a considerably more diverse crowd when again Patrick's remix was played at New York's legendary Loft Party. Amid the revelry I spotted two boys on the dancefloor wearing Patrick Cowley t-shirts, and I knew Patrick's spirit was alive.

Aside from his music, the journal arguably offers the most probing insight into Patrick's creative font. It is an affirmation that his artistry and his sexuality cannot be analyzed separately, but spring from the same creative force. His musical prolificacy already well established, why should these dual streams of energy prove much different? Josh and I continue to be astounded at the vast and diverse stores of his music that keep surfacing, thanks largely to Patrick's close friend and music partner, Maurice Tani, who saved countless tapes. Taken as part of his creative outpouring, the journal offers a unique window into an artist who never ceases to surprise even decades after his death.

By turns gritty, poetic, astute, and hilarious, Patrick's writing evinces an interior world as complex as the labyrinthine playgrounds he describes. His hedonism and obsessiveness, yearning and searching, delights and disappointments, his artistic references and inspirations, his aspirations and first gratifying tastes of success—they're all here, at times big and bold, at times between the hot and heavy lines. These are rendered all the more poignant by moments of transcendent self-reflection and uncanny foreboding, coupled with our own unforestallable knowledge of the devastation AIDS would wreak upon his life and upon that world. That Patrick's exuberant creative energy should come to such an abrupt end is perhaps the most fundamental shock, the one in which we can see our own mortality reflected. And so we must dance and revel, love and celebrate, and via his journal we too can be initiated.

AUG 18, '74
Lee on the top bunk
The marathon billiard game
(ticklin' the 'ol duodenum)

AUG 24, '74 Jim after the wine & fromage

MAY 10, '75 A rugged blonde bulldog beard You're like a bear lickin'
honey. Double occupancy wood paneled phone booth. *"Come Baby"*
– FSB –

JULY 18, '75 a peak experience
a lean dark honcho hungry eyes. among the mechanical fantasys
buggered up the ass. "Really man, …" and "It was." an armored
breastplate beneath his chest and me weak in the knees – TUBS –

AUG 10, '75 Fairgasm on my feet. Neanderthal on a bicycle who
took me to his slum and hung me up. His uptight vegetable rap and
my LSD patience. The painting of Archie must have been my recom-
pense. For 31 cents.

AUG 18, '75 the rescue. J besieged by obnoxo ----- and the Turk
turned him away. "take me in your arms" and he does. a shy kiss, he
is rewarded. keep your eyes peeled.

AUG 3, '75 That honcho again in the dim red light. Not quite so hungry. Took a generation with him anyway ¿ gave me a smile you won't soon forget.
TUBS

AUG 22, '75 The moon eclipsed by Slavic cheekbones. city sound coming up in waves. a shooting meteorite blazes into oblivion and punctuates the Perfect Evening. lustful, melancholy and a sense of impending separation. Michael Massachusetts, goodbye.

SEPT 16, '75 The cycle begins its renewal. Silky brush cut, blonde and beery gets down. The thrill of the checkered hunt. I bait. I wait. It's worth the tight suction and dramatic spread, veins bulging. Faces in shadows turn our way. The smell of his shampoo then out wheeling into the night.

SEPT 21, '75 All the stages of earlier evolved man, hairy & thick lay under my churning slipping hips crying "Oh, Man ... oh, MAN" I lay now, minutes after his footsteps retraced the hall, in a cool puddle, in rumpled white sheets smelling this man's unevolved armpits on my moustache. Aroma of Men. Hugo. This man. You've seen the same hairy sturdy knees in a Scottish kilt. He plays a double reed bagpipe. I want to fuck his ass to chanting bagpipes. I want to reach up under a kilt and close my fingers round his dark cock.

He wants to fuck me with his musical fist and see my juice shoot across the field of black hair that is his body. Short black hair is banging on my wall, his head, Hugo's head thumps when I thrust and a little boy's voice cries out low, cries out quick, "Oh, Man ... oh, MAN"

OCT 18–19, '75 My dark descendant of the Aztecs brings the smiling disposition, thick dark cock and fur covered lower half as well as the flashing Spain other half and together we toast the first 25 years of my life. At night, in the morning, later afternoon, on the floor or bed we fuck one another. When he leaves at 5:00 Mon. I remain amidst tipped glasses & empty champagne, strewn about clothing & smooth vaseline – Oh, look at that 25 year old purr!

OCT 20, '75 "There's nothing hornier than someone who's getting it." (Theresa McGinley) and ain't it the truth. So I see Ron across the room in the dim light and I call out with my eyes. We clench and press ourselves tight in standing embraces. Do you like to get fucked in other circumstances? Follow me. This curly head with perfect tits and big eyes I love as he slides a very rigid prick up my ass. I'm bent over the toilet or he sits on the seat and I on him, on that stiff smooth pole. Dirty love I say and I fuck his hard ass too – ooo we gonna do it again.

OCT 23, '75 The door is open. A bearded monkey man lies ass up on the bed. I touch him slow smooth working toward that ass as it slowly begins to churn. I close the door and we fuck deep and fast. He squeezes it out of me and we can only laugh… Later the coffee skinned work of art pushes against the wall above his head and I lift his tight and oval ass up and down on my eager dick till I cry for pleasure and fill him right up.

OCT 26, '75 Down at the club on the day we roll time back. Soon I spy two favorite beauties. Perfect Master I feels as firm and tight as he looks but a quick sweep of his brawny back is all I've earned. I take a cue from him, though, and chase black men all night. What a dream! The perfect, handsome, black skinned man who occasionally comes in the store is mine in the corner of the hallway. "This is the Rock of Gibraltar," I say, his solid ass caught in my palm. He groans so low and so real I'll be hearing it in my dreams. I finally do it - I kiss & lick that fantastic shaved and perfect skull of his. His cock curves right down my talented throat – He will come & take me home.
I spy Rigo up to something in a room but can't see for the black spectator blocks the doorway. He goes in & I follow. My friend is the bottom & Pal Joey the top. In a flash the four of us are connected. Much amyl later Joey & I work it all out. He wants a shower of piss & I can't seem to switch systems. I spank He spits. My hand is as hot as his black ass and he weeps as he shoots. I just don't want to be left alone he says as I close the door behind me. I had a ball I say & he laughs.

OCT 27, '75 Rush hour. A Texan & I between the blind mechanical fantasy flashers. He has frantic energy & very soon leads me away to his middle class flat where the quickie trick of the year goes like a blink. Whoosh & I'm stoned & fucked & on my merry gay way feeling time out of joint & juice in my pants. That midwest cocaine dullness can only leave a trail of discarded *bits of address.*

NOV 1, '75 I snuck over & charmed him away from the blow job he was getting. Charmed him to my bed with a talented ass. I want to see it in the mirror & it's so nice to see us riding it out – He's like a welcome monkey on my back – dark bearded soft stiff hair clinging like a baby to its mama. I spray a shot like July 4. He say *wow* – and go home.

NOV 3, '75 Latin lover – lay me down on your slick black sheets. My feet against your wooly chest. You are a banquet for my soul and body. I would shoot to Nirvana straight away if I should die with the back of my neck nestled between your furry thighs. We glance down at the tiny world from our lofty love and speculate at leisure.
"Life is so fine when Love is mine.
I can't go wrong … Love in song"

NOV 11, '75 Enough! You must be reminded, punished, even. Surely you will witness just what you need. First you must spend yourself in a leisurely way. Enough. Come in this room, I want it up your ass. Shut the door.
Slap Bang. Now, out. Kevin. Yeah.
So you witness subtle differences on your way home. Precise array. They can be truly beautiful, dressed blackly, there's a sight.
(I SENSED THE <u>ACTIVE</u> IMMEDIATELY) Piss or Shit, anytime, baby. Because demons are devils are angels are spirit and image to be witnessed. You are to be witnessed. You must be reminded, <u>punished</u> even.

NOV 12, '75 St. Michael & St. Patrick, their halos slightly a-tilt, made a real stir when they appeared to a small gathering of devotees tonight. Their dimly lit forms gave off a warm glow as they preformed ancient erotic rituals. One to another, both to each other, an offering and a sacrifice, the boundaries indistinguishable – one saint astride another, bent to his thrust, churning to a transubstantiate rhythm. Until, Speaking in tongues, erotic litanies and the tongues of flame grow hot and hotter – all heaven breaks loose ————

NOV 23, '75 Who is this octopus – this starfish all arms and suction. Silent type but traces of temerity shine through. Rocks off on an army cot – army shoes – in Castro uniform. An army of lovers did they say? Spits in your mouth no class, no nothin but traces shining. He might have held me this one, even after I say emphatically *No.* On my way out I see a painting with tentacles waving behind a chair. An octopus sure as shit.

NOV 24, '75 Rush Hour. Dim waiting rooms are crowded with expectancy. My back is to the wall & suddenly they converge on me purring & clicking – THREE ON ONE. I have to move it. A mustache with soft straight hair spots me & hovers awhile. He gives me deep throat & I branch out toward a familiar face. A pliable carved statue who moans while it's soft. I'd like to but I can't wait – can't wait – can't wait.

NOV 25, '75 So you thought maybe lust was hibernating for winter…
not so
I'm drawn to the vulnerable, smooth underbelly of my own particular group. In doorways, against walls, stalls, rooms empty save for beds or carpets or couches. Everything is stripped of its symbols and higher implications and reduced to the natural state. All night long the men walk the narrow halls and dark rooms. A small, subtle, yet distinct and compact ritual is performed again and again and again. Out all night runnin' wild.

NOV 26, '75 An afternoon sex-up. A curving mound under rivets &
denim & long blonde hair. I'm on my knees worshipping Phallus. All around me are the other similarly engaged. I feel the one-ness of our activity. Silent yet all things understood.
You are absolved of all wrong, my son.
Thank you, Father. Perhaps I shall offer these things up to the poor Souls in Purgatory.

DEC 1, '75 Across that familiar back room, in the full red glow I see a golden idol bent to buggery at the hands of a bearded gladiator. They are brilliantly naked. I am filled with a one-minded desire and instantly forget the partner who chose me. I join them and praise the sculptor who created this perfection. The gladiator comes and it is my turn. What a fierce delight. "I want to be fucked" he says. I heed his demand, and soon pour another load of juice into his perfect ass. Too soon. It takes a third man to satisfy this hungry blonde god and his moans rivet every attention.
Leaving, we walk together. Jim, Patrick – they hope they see each other again. Oh yeah.

DEC 8, '75 A cute little Irish lad – freckles ɛ̃ moustache and nifty little sports car. He would like to choke on it and I thought he would also liked to have fallen in love a little so I had to be a bit aloof. What a sweet little ass. Streamlined cock I could suck for hours, coaxing the come. Also ran: that man in the dubl-knit who stops off on his way home from work to purr over all the boys. Bored me, though. Some other time maybe, toots.

DEC 10, '75 What a beautiful dream I had last night. I was in a bed, high above the city. I could see a vast glittering panorama of lights below. I was in a warm bed, with smooth black sheets. I turned my eyes eastward and there lay next to me a perfectly carved idol. A beautiful, peaceful Mexican face with rich black hair and full curving sensuous lips. Dark eyes, rich brown. A brown mark on the right side of his forehead is like a reminder. It says "There is a treasure inside." And I say, "And there is a treasure outside as well."

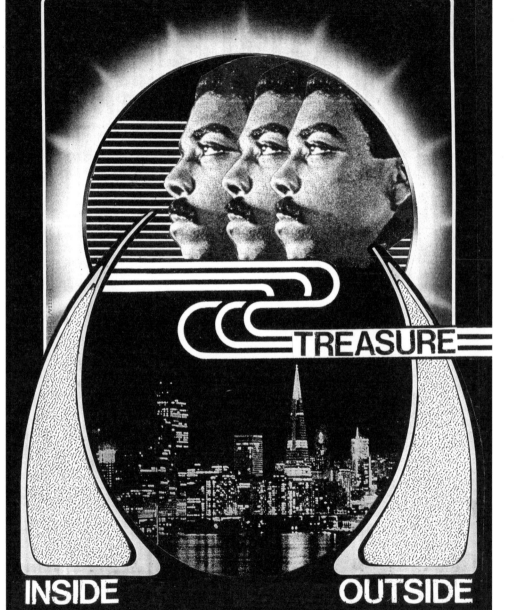

DEC 14, '75 A dungeon. Dull grey bars everywhere. a prison of choice. Surely the pit of pits. *Yet* I am not alienated by this littered filthy place. I feel a sense of easy familiarity. I know the façade and what lies behind it.

But I pick my way through the broken glass (bottles breaking all night long) and through the mostly tired fare. An Aussie chap keeps telling me what I should be. He's easily charmed – I enjoy doling out my replies. Inside the pit I tell him nicely, "Please don't be so insistent… it makes me think you don't understand" He acquiesces. Then a nice hunk sidles up and we vasser. Back ¿ forth. He's got a nice hand action he uses with his mouth ready for the reward. He's not let down. And he gets the same back – and gives me a bitter-sweet load just as the lights flash on signaling the last call – Made it in just under the line….

DEC 16, '75 Castilian Spanish ¿ *Mayan* blood flows in his veins. He stops abruptly gives an immediate, cocky come on. Rude Rudy. What a face. Solid, totally hairless body. "Are you a member?" … "cute member" … he's saying. Deep throat on knees ¿ he wants it in bed. He ludes me and I lead him here to my bed. Roll ¿ pose ¿ give ¿ take. We talk dirty. I fuck him twice. I get a standing fuck next morning, wacking him on those big thighs. Snugglin' up to that Latin look…

CHRISTMAS DAY – 1975

I
THE POPE closed a sacred door today
one that will remain closed
till the year 2000.

Bohemian Rapture Queen
and phased organs on the transistor, sister.
A lean muscled torso
peering from beneath
a high school sweater

II
For the past year a spiritual door has been open.
A door to the inner chambers of the Pope of the Roman Catholic
Church. I, being estranged from Holy Mother Church for a while was
unaware of this great opportunity

III
Beautiful Sins
The Pope's vision of what constitutes sin.
Cosmic Sin
National Sin
Genetic Incestuous relationships float by.
The hold, sexual hold, that women have upon men.

Arthur C. Clarke invented *Telstar* (The Tornado's recorded it)
His exact idea.
He invented Radar.

JAN 2, '76 Nicky takes me crusin' Christopher street on a bitter cold night. A fat burger at David's Pot Belly and a few beers at Kellers. That handsome Latin looker smiles and you know me. Nick & I wait for him and he leads us to Cell Block Speakeasy with a Suckroom and an almost uninterested clientele. Games go round and end where I knew they would – In a taxi headed for East 36th.

The Christmas stocking on the apt. door clues me in that I've mis-heard his name. Rolando from Chile.

Angel hair tree, Marilyn fascination (she's a Tool, always was, I realize) 19 crystal candle holders.

Delightful sex cause honey this boy had been away on a voyage apart from civilized peoples. Niño, that was real good sweet. You saved NY NY to me.

JAN 4, '76 Home again, Good ol' San Francisco… I'd swear the cabbie said. "Is that all, doll," when I retrieved my luggage.

Buffalo, a nice place to raise your kids up. Shopping sprees and burger joints at the mall. Sepia tint neighborhoods and the winter sky. Indian Orchard, Caz, Strickler's Hill – old names I once had use for. S & G said it well… "Nothing but the dead & dying back in my little town."

New York New York, so nice they named it twice. Hairdressers & chic chicks give glamour to dance in dumps. Debris & dinginess. I always spot check the silverware in those "fabulous" little places.

Teresa's ungodly hovel – catshit ironing board roach with an iron bar propped against the door and pigeons that sound like people copulating all night.

But those streets are the ones I've sung about. It's so old, so tired, so irresistible. On the subway you cannot resist. On the streets and avenues you cannot resist. In famous familiar sounding stores, restaurants and surrounded by all those anonymous people you are unable to resist the pull of NY NY.

I Hate it I Love it

I Love it I Hate it

JAN 4, '76 The Welcome Wagon was out in full regalia at the club tonite. These are my people. The small man on the bottom bunk with a sweet movement in his ass. Late comes main scene. That nice corner by the glory holes should be consecrated ground. I fuck the man in the box by just standing there. He makes the wood crack pounding his hungry ass onto my unbelieving cock … I explode. Before I've recovered his partner takes a stab at it. He's one of those familiar ones I've lusted after time ȝ again. He slides onto my half-hearted hard on for a ride. When the cutie in long johns shows up I've got it put away. He changes my mind quick. A long choker is my preoccupation for a while. Then I aim him for that incredible hole, knowing what he's in store for. He plugs right in, reaches over and guides my slow grower right up his nice ass through the crack of his long johns. In no time his pumping the asshole in the box has my cock up his ass ready to go again. But he lets loose his load before I catch up. After a time I step up to that hole again and Mr. Fantasy gets down on it with incredible mouth action. I give a practically dry come at this point. Welcome home baby.

JAN 5, '76 Steven ȝ I. He says we'll have to make it quick. A small group forms in the red light, flanked by those long dead mechanical fantasy boxes. A touch of popper from the bearded one and he slicks up to be fucked. I picked up on that one ȝ move behind him. Sometimes I wish I was taller ȝ this is one. Like a ballet I screw him on my toes, knees shaking from effort. The shorter, meaty man; good looking – he bends over and plugs into the man I'm doing. Steven on his knees completes the picture. 3 men come *pow bang zoom*. Like pachyderms in the circus' grande finale, one astride another, we roar out our pleasure. Afterward it amuses us to learn they are lovers. "We like to get things going" they say. "That's one for the Bicentennial" says I.
"Lets get together on our Sausalito boat where we live" – Well <u>all</u> <u>Right</u>!

JAN 7, '76 Café Niño… This man is an idol. The curves of his lips beneath that stiff dark moustache… liquid brown eyes nearly flat on his brow… smooth rounded forehead… Indian blood cheekbones and broad, noble bridge of his nose … These clench and tighten as he comes closer and closer to fulfillment there above me. He has me begging. Fast, furious and precise at times, he pushes that huge broad café cock into my ass and soul. This man is an idol and my eyes praise him when they set upon his face in the morning. Café niño, Jorgito.

JAN 9, '76 The box within a box within a box. These dark silhouettes are into stand up sex and have perfected a few of the more esoteric practices Socializing ξ Sexualizing one next to the other. You can be swept easily into one or two of the deeper corners where it's a quick transition to blow jobs or shower scenes. "I'd drink a gallon of his piss" he says and follows me around till those two beers are begging to come out. No way I can change systems for a shower in this guys hungry face. He gets come instead. Enough. Stevie ξ I head for the club. Many situations of different intensities here. That strange man Bill on the big bed, like a concubine in a harem. That wiry punkette who watches me pose in a doorway then leads me into that corner stall. Oooo he gets it up the ass for a while ξ that meaty cock of his double bound in rings and leather. Look for him again. Finally Jon the teacher and a nice prolonged see saw fuck, back ξ forth between us. The bottom bunk vibrates while Stevie waits. Pour that come spread across that familiar chest and sigh satisfied and sleepwalk home.

JAN 18, '76 So, Gary and the Glory Hole – both familiar to me these men. They have chiseled bodies ripe with definition – those tits, asses, jawlines… In the room we ride one another (I remember wanting a mirror) I pin him to the corner where the bed meets two walls. He's folded and flipped over like some vinyl lover half empty of air and he's moaning and gritting as curly head bumps rhythmically the wall. I can tell he's tired out — — — he's been on the battle field for hours, but I make him fuck me till he shoots that last wisp of a load – all nerves at this point. I tell him he's an inspiration. He was an inspiration.

Later… you know this one well… Next to you at the Café Flore with some secretary. A sculptor carved him years ago. The granite of his flesh yielding to time slowly but time is ever-relentless in its process, recess. But that's why I'm standing there in the doorway waiting and watching him working on that rigid one coming through the wall. He's the man I fucked up the ass through that very same hole a week or so ago. I'm thinking… I want to give it to him again… I will… I hang from two parallel walls that are so thin they cut into my fingers. I'm banging my prick down his much practiced throat. He's a receptacle of lust at this hollow time of the night. I'm a belated 4th of July rocket whose time has finally come… finally come.

JAN 20, '76 A neighborhood run tonite. I scurry in a familiar dark place. I see the mechanical fantasy boxes have had their power restored. That man smells like David with his lean sweat & patchouli. What a heavy veined meat he's rubbing up against that stiff bulge in my pants. This man is somehow like my jerk off buddies of yore. We do just that and come simultaneously. There's gobs of come everywhere. I'm chuckling as usual as it drips from his cock to my cock. A great pop. "It's Unanimous," says he… "It's Anonymous," says I.

JAN 23, '76 In a sewer, a shining underworld cave where a lost race fulfills an ancient prophesy. It is tropic as I bend into his rigid thrusts then back up and grind my rhythmically talented golden ass into his loins. Later, fighting the slippery cave surface, I pin a man to the steamy white corner. He smiles erotic gratitude. A smooth forthright fuck in spite of the atmosphere. We rise above it and then out into the cooling night.

JAN 25, '76 Sex Junkie… episodes in the further explorations of greasy Adonis… Finally, in the darkness of circling and baiting, the touch mouth rhythm and blond man-boy on the round foam platform. Live sex acts performed for your pleasure by real people… I am like a rare pet pleasant to the touch… I respond… I don't respond… I wait alert to your retreat. Later, I'm a child hiding. I create a scene… Hairy, only just discernable as light and dark. One more… say, "one more" more…

JAN 27, '76 That black bearded boy I watch. He's like a tense bow arched over that upturned ass of his partner. They part the boy offers his fine butt to the ceiling. Quick as a flash the studded, belted ape man mounts and rocks into it. I am diverted meanwhile by a mouthful of some stranger. Later black bearded boy is abandoned. I praise his body with my hands. I praise his butt with my hard-on. We have rhythm and the spirit moves within us. "Here it comes, baby." and I'm wailing in his dark hair. Sagittarius moon is satisfying if non-committal. Remember the feel.

JAN 31, '76 And another long converging circle closes to completion. Deaf John at Fred's New Year of the Dragon dinner and I stand around like a groupie waiting for grace. Georgie charms all nite but he ἐ Dana his roomie leave before us. Later, a miraculous summer night on the Street. Door to door sweet babies and John is spied, alone entering T.H. Georgie seeks but doesn't find and says "You go in ἐ look for him" ... "OK." I think I've missed him too when a tap comes to my arm. That arm is quickly circling his trim waist. Slip my hand into his back pocket ἐ squeeze. An affectionate kiss knocks my lens out of whack. He leads me to the mirror and flash we're sucking. In the mirror I see curly Lebanese hair plunging on my pole. I knew his mouth would talk this way. We exchange quick loads, me on my knees, He sitting on the can while I dangle from the wall ἐ sink. I guess I'll take what you steal from me John, you're a thief of love and you slip out the back into alleys and away.

FEB 1, '76 I met Joe in the glory hole room. What a hunka. He rubs his short-bearded handsome face in my crotch and worships Lord Phallus with his mouth. Later in my room (125) he spits with that mouth and it's like a sacred rite. The beauty of his strong back as it curves down to the glory of his ass brings low moans from me. "Fat cock"… I tell him, "shove it up my ass." "Oooo… a tight asshole." says he. We have control of this scene, both of us prolonging it till he says "Why don't we come." I tell him "slam that juice into me" and he does. My cum shoots all over my chest. Goodnite Joe.

Then it's that sweet punk boy Johnny. He wants to get me high. I like the way he sounds when I pinch his nipples. I like the way he swaggers around in his levis ¢ leather chaps. "It's for looks"… he admits, "not a statement of intent." "Give it to me" and I do for a while. He schizes away after 'luding me though ¢ Stevie wakes me hours later. I'm in a holy stupor and singing "Just like a Buzzin Fly." I miss Tim Buckley.

FEB 7, '76 Another dream. Prince Charming on the stage years ago. Tall, square-jawed man with long curling hair. He's stretched out long and solid on his back on the large bare bed. I stretch out alongside and watch for the searching arm to reach out for me. I'm not disappointed. A phallic worshipper whose devotions are precise, masterful. Later a smooth skulled man invites my penetration on that same bed and he's not disappointed. His long cock, not wide is unique. Hair grows, sparse but apparent right up the shaft of his prick when its hard-half-way along the length it stops. It's rough on the throat I conclude.

I end the evening with frustration though. The churning, crowded heat of men in a sexual banquet crowds in on me and the forced-by-circumstances emotion-lacking atmosphere drives me away. Away.

FEB 14, '76 Further explorations in the phallic-worshipping mastery of the Prince. He is silent, devoted, flawless. He glides by me as I pose, twisting the elastic band onto a towel. I feel his hands almost before I can imagine their reaching out for me. My ass, my belly, he slides and pets me – my growing cock. He takes it deep into his fine mouth and holds it there. We trade off the parts of devotée and master, kneeling in supplication, elevated like a saint on his pedestal. The light is like candlelight and the hallways are full of acolytes. The sacraments are offered up. We transubstantiate. We ascend into heaven and come all over the right hand of gods.

FEB 15, '76 Mardi Gras Party. David, a familiar face. F. Scott with his red hair and handsome face. We come from a similar lineage. A Barry Lyndon fantasy. He's well built with a fat pyramid cock that grows upward with passion. We neck and do the fellatio exchange till we're fired up. The others have to move over in this 3 story orgy, and give us a space to do our fucking. Oh Babe he moans as I slide into his appreciative ass. We rock on with this one, truly a classic. He lowers himself on it and rocks and churns. We inherit a bed and soon my growling is in their ears. This is a sweet sex and the feeling flows with the juices. Let the feelings flow. The longer you love, the longer you live.

FEB 20, '76 Games I play. The tall man with the faded forehead, a neighborhood face. He and I is the only sharp combination. *But he must ask me for it,* I say, remembering some past feeling. He does play by the rules and I'm climbing that dong of his, a tight tight fit down my throat. He guides my subtle teeth to his chest ₤ nipples and beats off moaning. This is how he likes to get it off. "*Do you want my load,*" he asks.
I drink that juice right down.
Inter-tracheal express load.
He pets, hugs and goodbyes.
Within seconds my come is flowing down the mechanical fantasy machine.
Remember this man's well hung ass.

FEB 22, '76 Two rogues, Irish rogues fuck supreme. I'm having a string of countrymen lately. Red hair, Light hair sturdy men. Tonite Michael ₤ Patrick pumping their bodies, their loins ₤ asses in rhythm ... horses ... horses ... horses ... He likes it deep ₤ hard ₤ fast. He is an inspiration. He's on his knees bent to my plunges. I'm on my feet crouched and fucking pushing grinding sliding fucking squeezing fucking his fucking asshole with sublime passion ₤ lust. coming crying coming crying out like an animal from Ireland. Irish animal crying coming out.

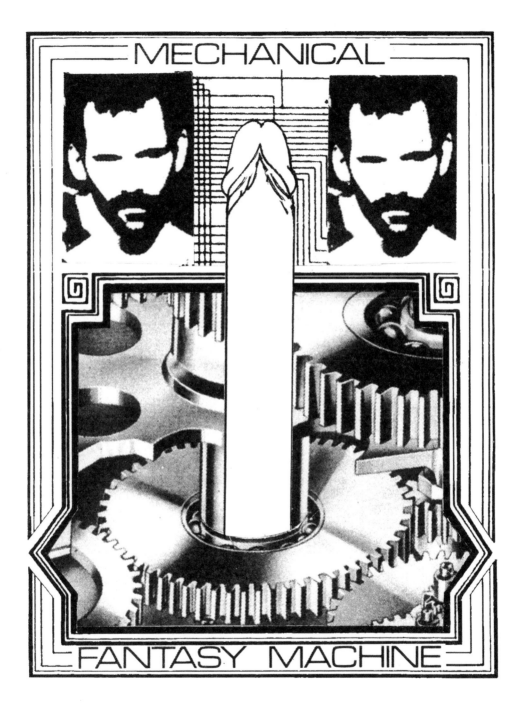

FEB 29, '76 Remember this: When I was 25 I possessed the cocky self-confidence of youth.

It seems that life is there for the taking and I took my share.

First there was the neatly bearded young man, Richard, who fucked me good but had little charm. He came as I beat him off, but only when he heard the guys in the next room slapping & moaning.

Then that blonde boy on the big bed. I balled him athletically for an appreciative audience, he blew me a kiss before he disappeared.

Finally that sinewy, lean, hair-thatched chest man who had the room next to mine. He would lope and pose and breathe like a fag in rut. Handsome, he liked to slap and spit and talk dirty. With his fingers up my ass I jerked off and fell back on the bed just as I shot my third load into his hungry mouth. "You can do that anytime baby," he flashed.

MAMA **MAR '76** *(undated)* opened tonite. The Baby re-members her Mama and bits of our mamas. She has distilled the poison within the bad mama and holds it up to see before being rid of it. Later I laugh and sit with two current mamas, Delores & Amber plus the Baby, Planet & Scrumbles over coffee (what else) and community and warm loud bohemia a la '76.

Broken Dishes next and *Pearls Over Shanghai* by October. And what of *Cobalt?*

Still warm from a weekend spent with Jorge Baca. That beautiful, this beautiful man has my heart next to his heart. I feel so beautiful walk-ing down the street with him ... sitting with my arm around him on the bus ... his eternal affections in doorways on sidewalks and lying in bed.

The fortune teller, *Percy Jane,* says I'll grasp the opportunities and really *GO. Percy, that's why I'm so far away.*

MAR 15,'76 full moon in a balmy night

MAR 16, '76 "Show him what kind of a man you are," a voice speaks to my left ear. I'm planting my 3rd load up that slim black man's ass. Earlier a bearded beauty and I suck each other off in the glory hole room and there I suck someone off and get fucked standing up at once. Tonite I'm often a receptacle and swallow load after sweet ¿ bitter load. My seed surges up two asses and I slide on home, a wharf rat after the party's over...

MAR 24, '76 Haunting the old dark places. Two beers ¿ a checkered shirt has 'em flocking. I've upset every mechanical fantasy box with my trying to keep balanced as the procession of cock hungry men kneels before me. My favorite, who's come was for me, was small ¿ dark with curly hair ¿ mustache ¿ a high school jacket. A perfect deep throat cock that got a royalle blow job while all the boys got off around us. Later that ass licker ¿ I beat 'em off together and smiled away.

<u>APR 1, '76</u> April Fool's

John with your long dark hair, square jaw, I'll have to write here what it was like with you. First that incredible marathon of fellatio your hard curving cock, upward, that I adored with my mouth face head that tiny rim of nerve mountains on the head of your cock. While sucking it I lean back and join your mouth ¿ mine with the man's coming cock – you ¿ I share his juice once then another comes and you fill your mouth with jizz and spill it into mine sharing juice twice *(I still can't believe you used the Trevi fountain image)* Sweet affectionate baby I finally give you an incredible roaring load, you fill your mouth and again spill the juice, my own, into my mouth... thrice.

And then later we're together again. I lead you into the room with the big bed where you suck me and fuck me so sweet I could die right there. What an incredible whole body LSD spasm of orgasm you gave me then. Holding you on top of me probing every inch of skin every dip and curve of muscle on that beautiful hairy body so good so good your lovely ass square in the palms of my hands. And your mouth was like novels to my mouth, they carried on incessantly familiarly and I said "our bodies are in love with each other." Sweet John It's good for me you disappeared, I was too willing to forget everything else but you and me John ¿ Patrick.

Goodnight with the fabulous smell of oranges and your spit on my hands. I'll sleep with my fingers up my Nose.

APR 16, '76 Prince C. and I together again. Never a word or sound from him. We do a nice act too. So this time I sit up afterward and ask What's your name?... Nada. He just don't want to make it real. I'll have to be happy with non-verbal communication. He sure is an exquisite man.

EASTER/APR 17, '76 After the Balle de Conjeo Steven & I are back again. Tonite's special was an Oriental, no, Mongolian young man with long long thick black hair, a chiseled face with bony angles and truly a perfect body... hairless, compact, strong, lean, muscular, smooth and clean. We give & take while Steven waits. Like a pearl diver he can hold his breath for long spells of cock worship. Hope to run across this godette again.

APR 23, '76 Daylight saved
Russell & I met at the dark end of the hallway. We were surrounded by walls & men making out. Tonite I was looking for a specific kindness and some lover whose focus was wider than one-chakra. He gave it to me. His ass was so nice to fuck, we ended it on the floor... the rug chafing my knees. Athletic screw I mount him from behind and ride and rut and ram and pop off so satisfied. Later I enjoy finding out the specs. He's the haircut I've been wanting too. I'll see Russell again.

MAY 2, '76 Saturday night at the club. Date night U.S.A. An all night affair. First fucked, rather languid by the sinewy dark Tony who Steven cautioned me about ("Weird scene with a dildo," he said) but I kept that energy at bay. He smelled like a man. Many small scenes followed, some exquisite, like the blonde blonde man in boots & levi jacket. A wonderful "Oh Man" scene with Terry the real estate man (expect to call him.) He kept up a running soundtrack of smut and affirmation.

Finally that amazing hot scene with Steven and Charley. What an exquisite form had Charley, lying there, ass up in the air at the edge of the bed, Steven pumping. Steven appoints me an accomplice by asking me to fetch his dildo (it was so late (5 A.M.) no real hard-ons were apparent) and the Crisco. Like the prestidigitast's lovely assistant I present the magician with his wand. I got so hot watching that dildo in Charley's square beautiful ass I fucked both he & Steven a bit (as well as the tattooed man next to us).

LOVE IS THE DRUG I'M THINKING OF.

MAY 18, '76 The "McDonalds" of the baths tells me I can't join my friends for the boys nite out. Cast out of their plastic Eden I head out alone to more welcome vibes. The club makes me feel like "home." My short hair look is predictably a big hit & I get flattering remarks & loving looks and objective adoration. Hanging out in my grey collegiate t-shirt I spy another one approaching and soon Jim Harris & I are looking like members of the same club. He's got massive hands and arms and is very affectionate but eccentric in specific ways. His limitations can be charming. His hunky body squeezes the air from me when he lays it all on me. He has shaved his chest hair, presumably for his visual pleasure when he lifts weights. I am Mad for his smells and his sweat is like nectar. "I'd like to work out with you & you could lick me clean." Every day babe? ....

JULY 20, '76 Welcome Back. A pleasant night at the Barracks... but it's Johnny I want to remember. A strange voyage of misplaced articles sought led me back after having been driven part way home. On this return I connect with Johnny. He offers me a ride home. Turns out he lives in those condemned gray Victorians a block away. He's checking me out. I remind him that we've met under stoned conditions but he's forgetful. As he drops me off he lets me know he's mine tonite if I want him. I'm too depleted though and an instinct tells me to decline. His face is great... his delivery... supreme... "We had a great time then," I said as I stepped out of the truck cab. He just crushed his sensual punk lips to mine. He's had nothing tonite.

"Awww... don't tell me that as you get out of the car..." he replies.

"Now... I've had sex four times tonite and I don't think you could get an inch out of me... Otherwise I'd be rarin' to go..."

"Well with the kind of night I've had I should just let it go..." maybe in LA..."

"So long Johnny"

"Ciao Patrick"

JULY 27, '76 At the lake with Peter & Jay.
"I like ducks in the wild, they seem practical and purposeful."
"But they're capable of meanness"
"Swans are so beautiful"
"But they seem more decorative & vulnerable"
"Swans are capable of viciousness"
"They have to protect their beauty"

JULY 31, '76 David, the courtesan, the professional lover. A relaxed friendly dinner date... He likes the music and my ass and knows how to show his appreciation. By the next afternoon he's pumped three loads into me and poured off a lot of sweat onto my rainbow sheets. smokes a lot too and I learn to love the taste of tobacco on his tongue (rough like a cat). What a positive reinforcement this man gives me... something I needed under my belt when I have to deal with Peter's clumsy inattentiveness the next day. I'm left with a couple songs and the empty conviction that he can't yet accept that which I have to offer. He needs it but can't accept it. David is so easy and Peter is so hard. A Libran weekend for sure. "Keep looking and Keep on cookin" ....

AUG 14, '76 Pete gives me a great fuck and a good song title *"A Wicked Tool"* or maybe "a beautiful piece of meat." He has stark, dark African design tattoos on his large forearms… a burr head and a beautiful ugly face. One of the Hot Flash partners. He loves the deep fuck I give him. He moans. He tells me to bite his tit off. Says, "It was nice to meet ya, pal." I says, "It was nice to meet ya, Pete."

AUG 23, '76 P.S. Thanx for yer disease.

AUG 24, '76 Terry ȝ his handsome, craggy face above me, his entire body pouring off sweat with the effort of sex. "I ain't never been fucked like this before," I tell him and it's true. He gives it all to me ȝ I can take it. I have to give it back and feel the balance of roles and it feels like seven eleven heaven pumping this man full of come —

AUG 25, '76 David ȝ I, freshly cured, dive into it again. We have a rhythm together, an energy syncopation. My cock slides forward to meet his ass sliding back. He moves it in harmony when he fucks me and we come together, tight.

SEPT 6, '76 Andy, the orchestra conductor. A long time coming this one – from when I first saw him till I first sucked him. All evening at Stevie's I was in a state of agitation with his presence. That hysterical horoscope told me I'd be in for a quickie and boy did it ever clock him. But what a great one. Jewish affectionate strong hairy... his cock was thick at the head, so incredibly thick I couldn't get enough. I didn't get enough and ended up beer in hand on Castro. Andy lit the fuse and I was still smokin when he was long gone. Let's have an encore on this one, maestro.

SEPT 7, '76 An incredibly balmy night in the old town tonite. Left to my own devices when the group ego flashed away suddenly, I eventually visit the old haunted bookstore. Some <u>hot</u> books by Target and a door open (because it was so warm?) encourages me to slide thru with an out of date membership card. It works. The tall hunk of man who gave me that hot, interested double take, and who I subsequently lightly rubbed my butt against when he walked behind me, he follows me obediently into that familiar, but altered back room (the M.F.'s are still there.) A long stand up scene evolves. He smells great, he feels good. His blow job was too shallow, his cock very nice. I come beating off into his mouth. He comes jerking it off sitting down and sucking. *YUM.*

SEPT 9, '76 The boy finally makes it in the park. Dipping under twist-ed tree limbs, sliding through loose sandy earth to those obscure nests in the brush. I'm quite intent on it today and stand, hard-on in hand. The grey flecked man says "come over here" ¿ I oblige. He's nervous though and unclean and it takes the red checked shirt, curly blonde man who was watching to do the trick. He's got a beautiful big cock and says, "Do you want to take it?" I sure do. Deep throat come injection and his hand has my juice shooting soon after. His cock, still huge after coming, looks great thrusting out of his open levis and that sight gets me off. "Thanks" he says and I concur.

SEPT 10, '76 Remember the guy in the mesh shirt at the Fair – We give each other the longing looks again and this time I walk right up. "You've given me a hard-on with your eyes" "Now you'll have to do something about it" – Joe does

Joe BARRECK

SEPT 11, '76 I'm at the peak of a cycle. Three nights at the City behind the drums does a whole lot for my ego. So many handsome men working there who make us feel welcome. Each night I'd go upstairs to the back bar between sets and give energy (and get it) to Gary the bartender. He began buying me my drinks and I noticed him in the back of the club Thurs. night watching the show. The third night I tell him we should get together and he says "come back up when you're through" of course I do. What a hunky dream is this man. French English German and much Italian. Wavy brown hair, handsome bearded face with that self-conscious chuckle. Perfect square body well worked on tits and tan, those always erect nipples smooth brown expanse of broad shoulders. He is a beautifully aggressive fucker and I listen to him getting it off above me, those small cries. I like sleeping next to him and watch his face and body as he lies asleep, with that peculiar snore of his; very soft and nice like someone scattering dandelion seeds or blowing out a candle. I lie awake the next morning for an hour anticipating his cock down my throat. I'm not disappointed and love his hips raised into my face, thrusting his hard on into my mouth – he comes and I come. – Breakfast on him at Sears where they make us wear those baggy "dinner jackets" to cover our sexy brown arms.

"See you in paradise"

SEPT 12, '76 Broken Dishes at the Goodman Bldg. and a great date with David at his place later, after a burger at the Grub Steak with Stephen (his ex) and Jorge. His apt. is spacious and cool whites and we have a good fuck on his rainbow sheets. When he comes, pumping above me, he says his whole body shuddered & he'd never felt that before. The next morning I once again see his bearded face turned sideways into the mattress, his broad muscular back and globe ass raised to my cock giving him those deep even strokes he likes. We come together and shower together & have coffee at the neighborhood spoon and bid farewell till next time.

Fifteen minutes later at the bus stop a cute young cruiser has it on for me and says straightforwardly "You're a very attractive boy … or rather young man." I can only smile at this point, Just a smile.

SEPT 14, '76 Cute little Chuck with the dark beard backs right up onto my cock in the orgy room. He followed me in and watched as I fucked someone else for a while. He <u>loves</u> to get it up the ass and I've got a lot of aggressive energy to spend. This boy can take it all, in every position, from every angle as deep and hard and fast as I can give it to him. He weeps and moans right before I come. I get my fist up his ass but it's too uncomfortable without the amenities (crisco, amyl) and we'll have to attempt that some other time. I'll say yes if that call comes to do it another time.

OCT 5, '76 Tuesday night at the Club Baths releases the orgone. Tension vanished with the help of Richard and his hairy ass. He lay on his bed smoking a joint black & bearded big thighs and coaxing his cock for me doing likewise in the doorway. My eyes to his crotch & his face back & forth. He loves the fuck he gets and so does the handsome Latino man who comes in and comes in my hand. I lick his jizz off my hand, bitter, and shoot into the flying A. Earlier in the dark a tight tight body bent to my pumping energy. A great fuck standing up. Where'd I get the bruise?

OCT 6, '76 David; such a hunky boy I can't keep my hands away from him and walking down the street, sitting in the movies, watching TV you'll find my arm circling his shoulders, my hand cradling the back of his neck. Seeing him every few days I never tire of him. He says the same is true for him and we enjoy each other's bodies loving-ly and lustfully.

OCT 9, '76 I'm reminded how penetrating and open a look in the eyes can be when Richard & I see each other. In a group, we walk home from the Disco, all loose from dancing, and his interest is as appar-ent as mine. "My bus or yours?" Later I'm very much into his perfect dancer's body, tight and beautifully proportioned. His rigid cock is like a smooth arrow and close to coming from the start. He fucks me so nice in erotic positions and we both come twice, thank you very much. Not much rest for Richard who's up 3 ½ hrs. later for work. Sure glad it aint me. I like this Boston boy.

OCT 10, '76 Down at the bookstore with Charlie & Steve
The check shirted, bearded black, tall dude I'm looking for is a hot one with come on his breath. He strips right down for action and loves it when I lift myself up and hang suspended into his blow job.
He invites #3, merely a shadow and starts working him over. He comes jerking off as I, on the floor, give the shadow with that monster cock a work over. I can't believes I can take this big fucker all the way but I do, time & time again. A great load he shoots & a pat on the shoulder and woops, I recognize the face as the light intrudes upon it. I'm sure I would have balked had I known, and I'm glad I didn't know who the shadow was. Later out in the yard a great standup fuck is taking place in the tool shed. I suck off the guy standing in the doorway for a bit, but get bored. Back inside I get off nicely through a glory hole. Arms up, hand hooked onto the partition, pants to my ankles my ass pumping with the pumping on the other side. Adoring caresses as I shoot are coming from the doorway dude whose come I spit onto the floor. He's very appreciative.

OCT 14, '76 Steven takes me to "Hotel" on a Thrus. nite. Like they said, the Barracks has resurrected here and some of the same spooks inhabit the freshly painted halls and rooms. The spirit is somewhat transferred too (including the stoned element). Anyway, first off the intense, Slavic blonde man with the brown muscular torso strides right into my room, wordlessly undoes my pants and warms me right up. He fucks me for a while but really can't keep it going and eventually withdraws. He reappears 30 minutes later dressed to depart but gets sidetracked when he starts making out with me in the doorway to Steven's room. He walks in and starts sucking Steven off. The sight of his luscious ass in blue jeans gets me into it royalle and soon he's naked and getting fucked by me. He can't take my pace though and a while into it he again withdraws. Wordlessly. Very nice. Later, after endless cruising I see Don arrive and enter his room down the hall from S & I. We both dig him. In the glory hole room when I'm trying to find Steven to drag him home I find him in a crowd of gropers & suckers amongst whom is Don. We eventually connect & he gets into me as much as me him. What a delight with mounds of brown curls a great meaty little body. We make out like starved teenagers and he gets off in a deep throat scene. We split only to reunite minutes later in a 3 way with that cute black guy whose been wanting me. Two cocks at once, Two on one cock, a great scene. Don and I are totally absorbed. Hope he shows up again.

OCT 17, '76 Richard calls me at the studio and we plan to meet at midnight. I sit with my Irish while Angela caterwauls and thinking I've been stood up. But he's been waiting next door, having confused the agreement. His friends are silly and I'm glad when Richard says, "what do you want to do?" ... I say "fuck" and he smiles ȼ tells his friends goodbye. What a night. Two hours of foreplay and fucking each other. I worship his perfect body ... a dancer's muscles in his legs, a weight lifter's chest ȼ arms, a boy's face ȼ blue laughing eyes, a mop of brown curls, freckles across his broad shoulders ... a cock like a sculpture, a blunted arrow aimed up toward his heart. He fucks me in his lap again moving me lightly with his strong legs. Face to face, embracing and screwing at the same time is a friendly way. Fucks me good in the morning too and sets me on my way purring contentedly.

OCT 22, '76 A log of wax burning in the fireplace, Groucho on TV, Patrick and Richard snuggled up on the couch – content by the hearth. A comfortable affectionate companion who can also fuck me hog wild. Amyl rushes and his dick slipping in and out of my asshole – we watch in the mirror. He fucks me as I stand on my hands, upside down – downside gettin' it good. He dances in my ass. Remember this boy how he looked with my Perfect Master shirt on. Broad shoulder and magnificent arms accentuated by the sleeveless style of the black tight shirt. I can't help but squeal with delight and tell him how hot he is. Mucho infatuation with Richard. He's light.

OCT 23, '76 Welcome back David. He's been backpacking in Big Sur with his new flame. It sounds like he's a bit wore out from his trip and his hyper friend. We listen to "Patchwork" and get stoned on home-grown. I love giving his muscle sore body a thorough massage, I love his socks on and those great cakes. (He'd rather be noticed for his eyes, but the butt's the forté. A hot hot fuck I get (been gettin it a lot lately – "Nothin hornier than…" What a great buddy.

Good Clean Fun at the Disco. Ron comes up & says "remember me?" He's thinner after his kidney stones & has grown a beard. His hyper energy is exciting and I'm glad to hear him say "my place or yours". He has a quick nervous energy in bed, a great cock and ass. He loves to fuck & get fucked. I love the scene in the mirror, the leather thong round my neck, his ass raised to my double timed thrusts, a very energetic fuck. But after the lust is spent this boy tends to float off into another place. Joe is warmer but Ron is hot.

OCT 24, '76 A day of nothingness with Baba leads to a restless need for a bit of adventure. Folsom street bound. First though, the Jaguar while I wait for A. to finish work. I love the tool shed out back filled with poseurs and sucking. The collegiate takes me on and I dig imagining him some BMOC at Niagara who I'm forcing to suck me off. He loves my attitude and I guess others do too as they flock around. But it's that deep throat guy I've sucked with at San Greg. who gets me off. I love my hand on his throat feeling the cock forcing its way deep, fuck that face. On my way but that dark haired dude pretends he's mistaken me for someone and then says, "You like old men, man? Cause I came on to you but I guess you weren't interested." I say I don't remember his advances (I'm sure he's mistaken) He say, "You like suckin that old man?" I say, "Listen, anybody who can give me a great blowjob like that guy is great, I don't care if he's 90. And you're real hot too, maybe next time." "Yea" he says with hostility. He imagines I've snubbed him in favor of some old man and he's plucked. Good. The pompous ego ass. A mighty offended jerk.

Later A. and I luded and slumming at the Bolt & Hungry Hole (The Toilets) A weird intense pissy scene at the Bolt (the shower bar I guess). Some rapid fire sucking in the toilet. I lift that G.S.Q's t-shirt so the accommodating pisser can get it on his chest and stomach. A warm wet boy perched on a trough with sucking and stroking all around.

OCT 26, '76 David & I visit Ron & Joe to play tapes. Much stoning and appreciation. Bob Bolt is impressed & will use some tunes in the bar this weekend (Halloween). Another fantasy fulfilled. The boys will be messin around in the dark part of town and the soundtrack will include me. David and I walk back over the hill in t-shirts eating Bud's. We watch night gallery and go upstairs to fuck after I get a raging hard-on sitting on the couch. I use it on his ass. I love to fuck with David as we are familiar. I know his stroke and can match it. I love straddling his ass at an angle while his head is pulled sideways onto the floor and he jerks himself off. Next morning we balance it off and he fucks me till I'm happy.

OCT 28, '76 Can I stand it? Every time I make it with Richard it's the best. His experimentation and control; His timing and the sounds he makes – but most of all his exquisite body inspires such a mad passion in me. After our first Amyl rush I felt our souls fall into each other. He said "if we get any closer I'll be on the other side of you." When I saw him at OCH's I was blind to anybody else.

"I only want to be with you"

We talked about our steady boyfriends next morning – his David & my David – he said we have a clandestine affair & when I said that wasn't quite true, that some people knew he said "yeah, but they don't know how good it is." Well I know how good it is and I want to keep it up as long as it feels good. Boy, does it feel good!

OCT 29, '76 Well they can't all be heavenly right? Mark's party includes predictably quite a few male homosexuals. Doug with the Marlboro look is my pick hit of the party. We slowly give each other energy all night. Later a troop of us heads out to the Bolt to witness my Folsom St. music being played there. I meet up with Kevin Murphy who I first met at the baths. He's friendly (and complainant) and I'm torn between putting energy into him or Doug, who has now arrived. I make the wrong choice and go home with Kevin. He's uptight in Catholic ways. I don't like his selfish technique, his Gregorian chant, his coffee or him in general. Just his looks and that can't carry it off. When I leave next morning from his Pacific Heights single I'm glad to be rid of his presence though I carry the grey mood around for hours.

OCT 30, '76 It's the night before Halloween and the party's going full swing. George is an amazing speedball vampire and I'm a make-shift cowboy. James' party is a snooze and Georgie and I head back to Castro street. Much to my delight I run into Richard and crew (Billy J.) we end up getting stoned together with Gary Younger as the mad costumes and cruisers float by never endingly. Richard comes home with me (two nights in one weekend, oh boy) and it's an evening to make up for last night. The most interesting facet being my faithful six-shooter (Janet's vibrator) which we fuck each other with. An amazing sensation. Every room has the sounds of love making coming from it tonite. The dormitory is full. Next morning Richard ¿ I lie in bed for hours stoned on Thai stick and he makes me do a double orgasm with the vibrator up my ass. A humming way to start the day!

OCT 31, '76 Halloween night 1976 is actually a spooky affair. I watch Archie shoot up before we go to Polk St. (as I had watched Georgie the night before). It looked very unsanitary and unsavory. Polk St. is amassed with revelry and by the time we get there the lunatic fringe is taking over. Archie ¿ I dressed as cowboys in leather. I feel like we're milling about rather aimlessly and soon enough head back home. I want to make the scene at the Jaguar before it closes. I run into Richard again ¿ get stoned with him but we've seen enough of each other for one weekend. The bookstore is pretty quiet in spots. I look great with my darkened moustache, black hat ¿ jacket and boots and still packing my six shooter ¿ holster. Weird queens in drag in the darkness. Finally the blonde hunk in mesh and makeup loves my roughhousing. After a great load down his throat he turns my face into the light to remember me again. Hope he jumps on me next time he sees me.

— — — — —

Kaith?

NOV 1, '76 A neighborhood run tonite. I'm a nocturnal prowler and can't settle down at night till I've been out in the streets for a while. I meet another Richard --- blonde, craggy featured, trim. Right off he's assertive and erotic. Great mouth that offers a silent communication. We suck cocks asses faces necks muscles tendons in the room of mirror slabs that reflect only the dim dark silhouettes. "I want to do this in bed" and he complies. We walk up the warm streets home. Right off he's assertive and I could wail with erotic fantasy when I remember his form standing up above me on the bed, his foot coaxing my groin as he jerks himself off. His come spraying all over me, he pushes his spewing prick into my face, come smearing my face and I let it fly the way my brain is flying.

NOV 5, '76 Friday nite. A. ¢ I hit the streets luded and looking for trouble. No trouble finding it if you know where to look. The BOLT is the heart of Folsom St. The best tits in the world on display. Buddies by the barful, beauties, butch, bulky. The bathroom is filled beyond capacity. I spy the sloppy man, bespectacled, walrus-mustached whose enormous cock I remember from our brief encounter years ago. I grope him ¢ he responds (vaguely) I'm not mistaken. This man's unique tool is so fucking fat at the base I literally can't open wide enough to get my mouth around it. Fabulous load pulses into my mouth I swallow it like water from the fountain of youth. Soon after I'm standing with my dick up some stud's loose ass while he gets sucked off. "Breakdown" comes on the speakers and I'm at the controls once again.
All MINE!

NOV 15, '76 These days I cannot perceive things in quite the same light as previously. The finite nature of our physical bodies is made painfully apparent by David's accident. I feel fragile, like a Japanese house or a piece of lace. I am touched in a very deep and sensitive place by the people around me... David, Richard, George and Steven --- Some of the men that mean much, they are parts of me I don't want to lose. But I am reminded not too gently that other forces will make their power felt beyond my conscious efforts to endear and be endeared... to inspire ε be inspired to probe and develop and ease the pain and to serve as material to others for similar exploration. To love and be loved is a simple thing, as simple as life and death.
I am growing.

NOV 24, '76 Circles turning one by one... Circles converging not a moment too soon. The swan lands me a job as a spotlight man at the City Disco. Take my quarter down to the Jaguar to celebrate. The chunky short Latino man flips that big dick out and says suck it, man. Nice but incomplete. Now he wants to fuck me... I tell him to suck me off ε he balks "I don't suck" So I balk "I don't get fucked unless I get sucked" and that's that. Later the trim young man with light hair and heart-aimed hard on. Nice blow jobs in the striped red light. His warm come spurts down the back of my throat and I want to cough. I want every drop. He jerks me off and fingers my asshole – what a thrill, my come is flying all over. Some dude from the dark reaches in for a few final strokes and its out into the night.
Tom Cattin'   Tom Cattin'

NOV 25, '76 Thank you, Almighty One, for the orgy of input. Timeless love over the wire. Ties of time brought together under one roof ε lavished with the finest victuals and enhancers of temperament. Later, out into the winter night to connect with the others, the brothers. First John, on his back, a fine ass greased for me to slide in. Then Mr. "you're-the-best" weight trainer with the Apollo's girdle – common on short people, says he. A marvelous vigorous physique. Finally Tom and the bushy dark mustache who watched at first. We square off, trade off… he blasts his come down my throat, up my nose…. then I, using his come, jerk it off while diving into the thatchet of armpit hair and aroma. I come in his mouth.. he takes every drop ε drops me off. Thanks Thanks ε thanks.

NOV 28, '76 Jeff and Lucy. VITAMEATAVEGAMIN. Two hours in front of the TV/hearth with my dark haired friend…. cuddling and lounging on the floor with a roomful of the boys. Later my blunt "Let's go upstairs ε fuck" put out his romantic glow and he says his sexual energy is low. So I suggest we just lie down and feel close. He gives me a marvelous massage and talks on and on of some of his international adventures as a practicing homosexual…. Bringing a high school boy out in the South… anonymous sex in Paris beneath Notre Dame… a sex park in London… all of which continues to get me aroused and as we all know in men arousal is contagious. So we have a hot fuck after all. His nice prick up my ass gives me an orgasm from within, without a stroke to my cock I shoot it all over my belly as he fills up my ass with his warm moaning load.

NOV 30, '76 The boys club on the local street tonite. Loads of yuks. Later I head on over to TUBS. My usual careful wait for that one or this one. The dark Latino looking (Italian?) man with the glasses I like. I place myself in proximity and he is drawn straight to me. He's the perfect partner for a place like this. He's direct, strong and passionate, likes deep kissing and such. He's into the threshold of rough and me too. Pulls my balls, pushes into my groin, slaps my ass, sucks and jerks me off furiously, then gently. I devour his nice cock while pulling his low hanging balls down. He chucks a load pulsing into my mouth. He gets down on his knees to me, laying back on the leather covered spool table and I blast my hot load into his hungry fast mouth. Much hugging and holding after and a few words of appreciation after and it's back on our own again.

DEC 2, '76 It's a small tool shed out back. When I step inside the darkness I see maybe six men. One man is getting off moaning as another on his knees sucks his cock. Next to them a chunky bearded man facing me and bent over is getting an even energetic balling from a young mustache man who moans "Yea… Yea…". When the guy getting fucked sits up and back onto the cock (fat ¢ uncut) I can't resist getting involved. Soon I'm feeling that pushy sexy fucker's balls and hairy ass as it bounces into his partners. Then I'm standing on the platform getting head from the big boy while he gets it up the ass. A threeway. When I'm fucking his slippery ass he leans back from the suck job he's giving ¢ says, "He's willing and I'm willing and if you want we'll go to my place and you can both fuck me at once…" I whisper, "I have to go to work", and shoot my wad up his ass.

DEC 6, '76 DISEASED

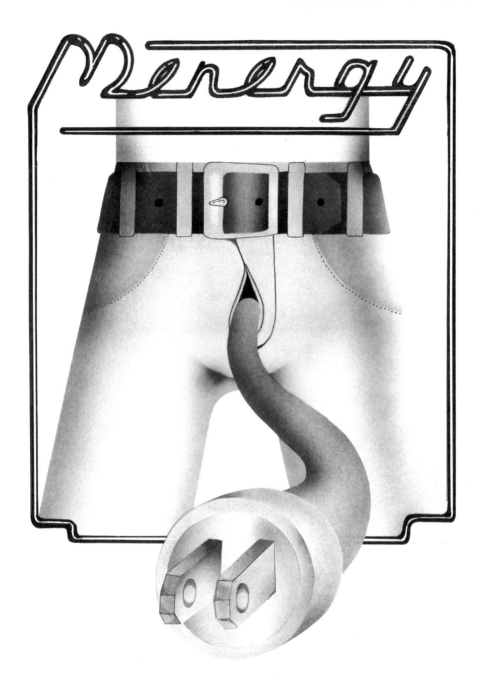

DEC 6, '76 The full moon pulls me, post Gotham, to a small unlit shack. There I meet a young man with the silkiest ass. He tousles my hair as I kneel before him. Much affection and home.

DEC 10, '76 Sipping champagne with Jane Olivor backstage. Her performance & Tom's booze sends me out to the baths with high energy to spend. First I connect with dark Larry. We suck together & cuddle on the top bunk. He has hairy balls. Later, after seeing the swan, I meet Charley who has a thick blanket of man-hair on his chest & belly. Handsome, with an awry smile always playing on his face, he gets trashy in the steam room. He spreads his legs wide and sits on my cock. But I want it completely in comfort so I lead him down to the bunk bed. There I fuck him so nice, just what my follow spot back needed to loosen up. He gives me a ride to the house, parks and we talk. Eventually sex rises up again and he comes in. We cuddle and he fucks me before I see him off into the early morning light. The sky is an ember as I close the curtains on a fulfilling night.

DEC 16, '76 Beautiful. What a shelf this one sports with his left nipple pierced through. I suck and lick and flick the small gold ring rapidly to his moans. Remember clasping his fine man's body to yours, feeling his shape, ass to shoulders, as my mouth inhales licks sucks pets tongues the soft thick bush of his armpits. Remember this curly brown pit hair nestled beneath your tongue and carried home. He lays out on the altar and soon, with my hand filled with his buttocks, he roars and pushes that mouthfilling load of warm come to me. Two, three times I'm full and tasting it. A sweet sweet mouthful and away…

DEC 19, '76 Remember… there are times when nothing is wrong but a feeling is there that makes you like a snake itching to crawl out of that tight, inhibiting old skin. So make it come lose. Snakes rub against rocks… I rub up against other men. Half-luded, icy gin and Brent-tonic, beer prop, home grown. The Jaguar afterhours. First off an anonymous hard prick gives me a full load. Then I corral a blonde Western boy, a bit held back. Waiting. There's that guy again. Seen him here before, posing maybe a bit self-consciously, showing us through that tight white T-shirt the weight lifters physique he works at maintaining. A sadistic angel. I think specifically of him twice… "He's more pretentious (with plaid shirt stuffed into his back pocket) than I am" (with my strap T-shirt and red hooded sweatshirt and coconut haircut. Then I think, "I'm afraid of (approaching) him" This admission wins him to me as a reward. He walks directly up to me and strokes me. I pause and caress that fabulous chest; hand, warm, hairy, packed into that shirt. His crotch is packed too… into a jock strap and cock ring. Much communication with our mouths and hands. He gets me off so hot sucking at my pumping hips. He's down ε leaning into me… I'm crouching low, back to wall, into his face. I tell him "you deserve this load" as I pull up his shirt and clasp those two pectorals in my hands. "Here it comes baby." <u>Wham</u> into his hungry mouth. On our way out I say "That was very satisfying". "That's <u>good</u>" says he.

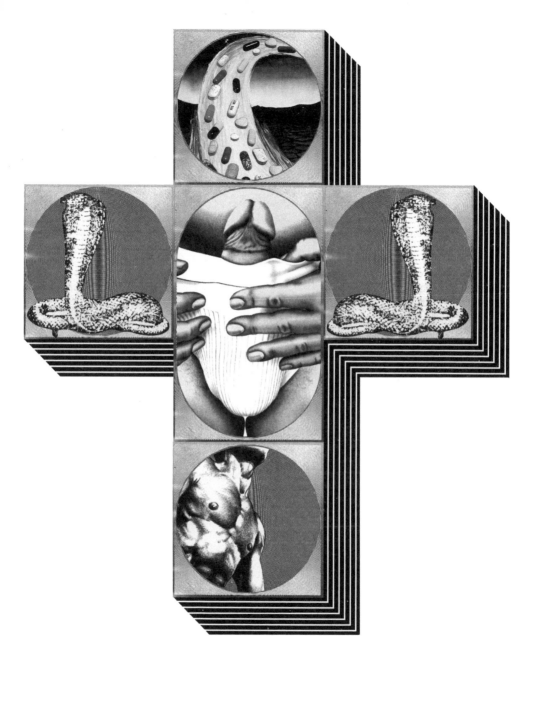

DEC 20, '76 A nice date with Jeff tonite. *Broken Dishes* and him laughing into the crowded room. No startling revelations. Just the quiet strength of companionship. Later we take Theresa back to La Playa and talk on. Then back to my bed. It feels like something long lost has returned when we embrace skin to skin. I love it when he slicks down between my thighs and fucks the place, his butt swooping smoothly up & down. Soon I'm in that butt and when the time comes he shoots into my mouth and I, his juice dripping from my lips, shoot my tensions up Jeff's ass. Next morning I say I need a dick up my ass more than whiter teeth and Jeff does me good. Breakfast at Hopwell's and we're on our separate ways. See you soon.

DEC 25, '76 A Christmas cantata at Valencia Street in the evening with Jeff. He is amused. Later, back at his icy back bedroom we overlook the chill to fuck. A great mutual orgasm, his cock up my butt. Some treatment in the morning and into the day.

JAN 3, '77 A week of trundling back & forth to S'mento leaves me only a quick visit or two to the Jaguar to keep me calm. This time that sweet young boy laid out like an offering on the altar. I work lovingly on his smooth cock 'til he shoots me my reward. Then he pulls me on top of him and I fuck his face. The great healthy smell of his sweat on my hands gets me off so much I want to carry it with me for hours afterwards. Much caressing and then... gone...

JAN 4, '77 I was tailgating John in the CB hall when he abruptly reversed his course and walked into me. His nervous apology gave me the power ẹ a few minutes later we're stoned and prone. His cock is wide ẹ flat shaped. He has smooth hair on his shoulders and on the small of his back. I have him fuck me as, true to my impression, it's my show. He pants like a puppy and later in the light I see his face is a mirthful one. Sucked off later in the catacombs of Paris by a brown adorned man. I love his face crushed to my abdomen ẹ balls while I jerk off. Then before I go back out into the quiet night I respond to the bearded blonde man's advances and fuck his sinewy butt with delight. Tonite the successor to my well traveled first cock ring was purchased.

JAN 10, '77 White come ẹ black cock. When Michael comes I take it in but then get the urge to see if his come is white. I fantasized it would be black like his strong sweet-smelling skin. The white gobs of jizz I stroke out to the tip and lick off. Handsome Michael (I wonder if he recognized me from numerous street group encounters) has such soft wavy hair for a black man. It attracts me a lot. His chest ẹ stom-ach furry soft. He sits up and works me slow at first, mouth and hand till I come with shudders and small moans. He drinks it in. He winks. I came ẹ went.

JAN 12, '77 A delicate (fragile) time in the back room. Heated up then doused with a wet blanket time ξ again brings out my claws. At one point I suck off for a long time some faceless dude with those rare tiny bumps of nerve endings around the rim of his prick (like David Cumming's). I want every drop. Finally get mine off standing on the altar while the hairy dark big man sucks me well. I tell him to soak that juice right out and grab onto those big hairy tits of his and slam it home. Nice...but the mood was not jubilation. My diet of Big Mac's in the dinge is not a nutritious one and I can't live well on it . Keep cookin' ξ keep on lookin'....

JAN 13, '77 Smooth ass Bernie watches, waits and walks over for a grope. We're in the subterranean workout room. Tonite I just feel "so what". I jerk off in his mouth. He offers me a ride home in his fancy big mobile home-type van. I'm amused as he launches into a demon-stration of all modern conveniences – sink, fold out bed, spice rack... Tells me he just bought a mansion off Dolores Park... I suppose he did. He gives me the data to date him but I know its no go so I throw it out ξ say so what ....

JAN 15, '77 N-Judah to Divis and the guy next to me on the bus asks me home. On the couch we strip each other for some rich oral action. Then to the bed where my fist ξ fixture explore his big ass. Amyl and assholes. Ron Reamer.

JAN 16, '77 Jerry and I smile and nod hello from across the café. He is so good looking I think about him all morning. I have to go back ¢ talk to him . He says <u>yes</u>. My guest in the booth for "Madame" is a well-formed dark haired mustachioed young man of *LATVIAN* descent. Mirthful eyes, intense affectionate. In my bed he moves with me. He steals my show both at night and the following morning. First time Jerry holds me back and makes me watch the come flow ... next time I take it as soon as he gets it for me. Casually grooming my back I see him in the mirror going over me where he says "This could be the start of something big."

JAN 17, '77 The long anticipated and hoped for call comes the Mr. Richard is back in town. How strange: the coke I'd saved for his return had been done the nite before ... *jinxed*.. This buddy is my fave rave. If the Lord takes me when I'm with Richard, it's straight to Godhead for me. We talk ... his enthusiasm is infectious ... his presence magnetic to my senses ... he makes me laugh and moan and tosses me around on his arrow perfect cock.
In the morning beat off with his come ¢ cock in your mouth ... looking up to his sculptured butt rising away from your face ... his healthy tits contoured above your tense, soon un-tense, self and body below.

JAN 19, '77 Jerry in the light booth watching Maxine Weldon. My buddy, affectionate… I can't believe he's 31 years old… Such a bunny. Our second night together; for sex I fuck his beautiful little butt. He can take it all and he loves it. Next morning he fucks me a bit till I shoot come all over his belly. "I love an audience" he says as he jerks off. A nice leisurely breakfast is my treat next morning. A real find is this man.

JAN 23, '77 Bunny

FEB 3, '77 A sunny Castro day. Baba ¿ I do our neighborhood errands. We stop to *fumer un* joint and the blood begins to heat up. A quickie before rehearsal with Morgana King today. Jaguar back workout room. Rick and I do the dance and connect. I'm feeling Hot horny hung ¿ hunky with my cock ring on 2 and my new jock strap. Rick's already hard when my hand strokes his crotch. I unzip ¿ pull that sweet long prick out ¿ shove it right down to my heart. His butt is in my hands, he fills me with his comeload. Much affection and I give him mine. Later on the bus I take out that little slip of paper and see he lives on charming ol' Pemberton street. Lookin' forward to a night or two up there with Rick ¿ his sweet sweet dick.

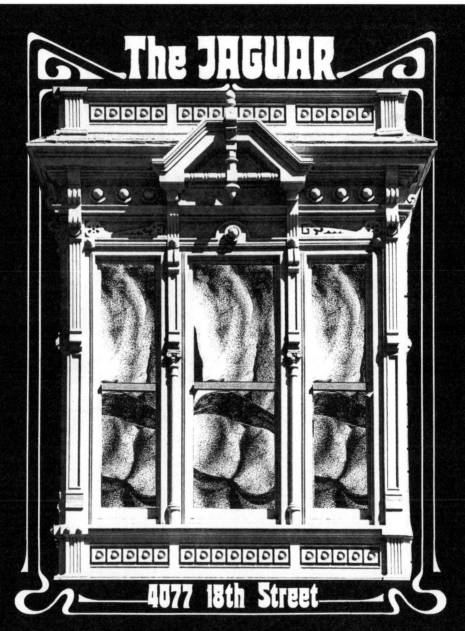

BATHS

FEB 4, '77 No junior high dance tonite. Restless eve takes me high to discover Jim in a dim corner, like a rare bloom in shadow this boy. Thick curly hair, thick dancers' thighs, natural cock that loves that deep grip of my throat. At home in my bed covered with blue light we carry on for hours. We hold me at the edge for the longest time… Give it to me hard says Jim as I bugger his sweet ass. Superlative full moon fuck.

Later a swell spaghetti dinner with some of the men… a cup of fresh coffee on the couch with Jim under my wing. Ending a beautiful Saturday morning with mine ¿ Janie's beautiful music….

FEB 19, '77 A peak experience. Peter Leone ¿ I go to a new baths after Janie. In a small room labeled "Zoo" I meet Marion Mora, dark beauty of German-Mexican descent. Our caresses become more and more intense as barriers are perceived ¿ dropped. I am reminded of Jorge Baca. Marion and I on display in a cage. Making loud love behind bars while people crowd around and watch. Occasionally a spectator reaches in to feel but I vehemently grab his hand and thrust it away. Mine. Marion's feet push against metal and his ass is raised to my thrusts while he chants Patrick Patrick. I sit on his cock, boy it's been a while. Dripping sweat, salty deep kisses tongues ¿ soft large Spanish lips brown deep eyes that are always a little at odds with the large smiling mouth framed by a thin black mustache. Remember his dark haired, thick forearms, his long cock and warm voice. More please…

FEB 23, '77 My second date with Marion, in front of a fire and the TV. Later he loves the music and we make out warmly, passionately, completely. Upstairs we're together, our bodies have a magnetic energy all their own. We fuck & suck each other for hours and finally drift off fulfilled. This is a special man, relaxed, quick to be amused and very affectionate sensitive and sexy. A winning combo. More...

FEB 26, '77 The incredible Bill. Latin with a South American accent, smooth and muscular he catches my scent and follows. Amazing. Sleeveless black and blue jeans low moans as I catch my breath and dive. To his room where the Latino macho fucks my ass with a steady smooth rhythm. I want it and get it face to face as we shoot together.

FEB 27, '77 I see Bernard's muscular body bent over the platform, his ass getting banged rhythmically. He's making noises. I get closer. He reaches for my bulging blue jeans and strokes. (Wham into his ass.) I stand between him and the table. He encircles me with his arms, strong and sweating, like he's got hold of a tree trunk. I make his sturdy back and arm muscles feel my hands and I hold him firm under the onslaught. A crowd. Suddenly he's up and gone... I want him. I follow him and put my arm around him. "What can I do for you?" "Catch your breath." "Do you want to go out to the shed?" "Too cold, let's go to my bed." I fuck Bernard up down & upside down and come shooting up his sinewy butt, my hands full of his solid tits. He maintains a jovial attitude and that's nice for a change.

MAR 4, '77 Stoned on hash, a balmy day with my boys. Wake up with Jerry, my bunny boy & join Arch and Jorge for café. Lunch date with Marion. Later, après hashish I stroll to Buena Vista (after Jerry's story of two mornings, 7:30 AM, getting fucked bent over a tree) It's a *primal* experience, stalking & being stalked. Who's this? That cute face is somehow familiar... I nod hello & smile. A few steps and I see him pause & begin to follow. I wander slowly down the path till he catches up. "We've met before" He says so too but it's a mystery where it was. Randy & I slip into the bushes looking West into a gorgeous orange sunset. Two curved hard pricks flash out of their jeans and into our mouths. Two good cock suckers hiding in the bushes give each other a juicy load of come well earned. See you Tuesday? Randy F.

MAR 4, '77 Full moon in Virgo finds me receiving everything I need. Last night fucking the man in the stall room of the Jaguar, my left foot in the window sill, right on the floor slammin and grindin my prick up his hungry ass. Tonite, gung hay fat choy, I suck off a neighborhood cowboy "Want to come to my place... two blocks from here..." Then Manuel & I dance slowly to each other. I work his Latin cock over good till at last he pumps it way deep into the back of my throat... so good, so good. "Remember my face" I tell him...
"Hello Dominic"... How ya doin?"... "Good"

MAR 9, '77 Mad hip grinding action on my neighborhood run tonite. Coked ¢ Hashed from Balcones ¢ Robert, positive energy abounds. A conga line of fuckers, when one drops out the anonymous ass backs right into me. He gets it all (I could never take the fuck I give) standing up. I almost drop from the rush.

MAR 11, '77 Jerry came in while I was finishing up my shower this afternoon. He stuck his head in the door and stuck my cock in his mouth. His hair got wet and I toweled him off while he worked me off. Sweat dropping from my brow onto his head, I finally let it go into his mouth.

MAR 21, '77 What a romantic evening was in store, was actually trekking across town on foot while I unaware lay abed studying the music. First a bump at my window … the wind? then another, a clod of earth on the pane! There stands Marion looking up, a smile from ear to ear. Before I know it my bed is occupied by this handsome dark haired, broad shouldered, bare chested smiling man, his arms, those thick, hair covered forearms and large wide hands hold me tight. I am falling into these deep-set brown eyes I am surrendering sweet surrender sweet … I give him my ass, I take his cock and we roll and moan. I shoot a long shot of jizz into my hair. I am humming with pleasure from head to toe, inside and out. I am surrendering sweet surrender.

APR 22, '77 I find myself in a big brass bed with a friend that I re-member thinking of, the first time I saw him, as a certain pinnacle of male beauty and desirability. Robert wearing a black leather and steel halter in the Barracks leather shop. I stood unseen and watched him move and attributed much inherent power to him. Last night symbol-ically he shot a load of power deep into me with his huge cock. Down with blinding mythology; replaced by equality and mutual apprecia-tion. But Robert can stand for an ideal of self-love manifested through body care and attention to the needs of spirit and animal.

APR 28, '77 David says "One thing for sure... you've got a great mouth." I rev up to "It takes inspiration.", and...
His tight lean torso and his lust to shoot that load down my throat. Bent over a table I take that fat cock of his. Clean off his prick with my throat.. I choke on it but will not stop... he fucks my face with a great attitude, slaps me 3 times, harder each time, in the side of the face as I take each thrust and try to breath in between... My main thought Give me that Come. Shoot it down my fuckin throat. He feels stiffer and fatter and can I keep it up and he fucks faster and holds my head and moans and fatter and quicker he comes wet thick in my mouth throat face I shoot it. David's Patrick's

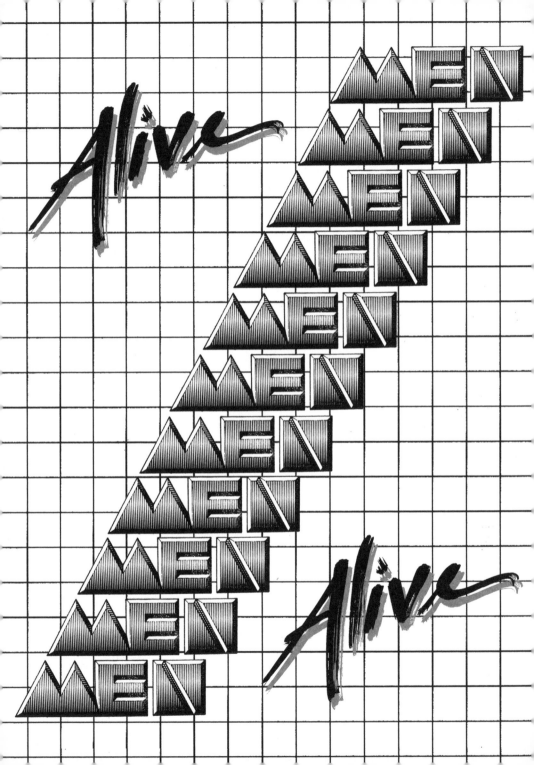

JUNE 4, '77 Weeks go by... New York Andy at his E 26th st. place....
Tom in the backroom of the International... Carlos Jones at the
Everhard... Johnny Green and his inflatable toy... Back in S.F. with
Jerry at my place and his... Marion here and on Russian Hill. Today
the tall one with the tight satin shorts ¿ jock ¿ cock that fills my mouth.
I suck on his hairy balls (remember the Italian guy at the Everhard
"suck those hairy balls".... "ciao") while he jerks it off for me to take. I
spit in his hand and he jerks me off with a blast...
My boys......

JUNE 6, '77 Mr. Norman's back. How great to plumb the depths of his
big hairy asshole again. Balling him hard as I can on the dope dealer
rug reweavers' bed in front of the mirror. Later a hippie cowboy ambi-
sex party at the country bar. Clean sheets ¿ Mr. Norman.

JUNE 13, '77 The night off. In the book store I get into Tom o' Finland stories in multi-languages. Exaggerated charcoal men in lumberjack and leather piled 3 high in fuck-chains. Too much... Farther inside B.D. ¿ I share a joint while watching a sacrifice. The men, 8 or so, stand around the room ¿ watch the leather platform. The man lying down has his work boots on but no pants. He's getting a fast rhythmic fuck with his legs overhead. The top man in tank top ¿ mustaches stands straddling his partner and holding his legs at the ankles. Men look on. Stoned now I get up and walk over behind the fucker. I watch his ass and my hand slides down the hairy globes towards the fur of his asshole and beyond to feel his balls slapping against the fucked man's ass.

I meet the thrusting ass with my hard on in my jeans. I bend down and slide my face into his hairy butt and my tongue into his sweet smelling hole. I plunge in and he still moves to the rhythm of his fuck. I go down under and scoop up his hanging balls in my mouth and feel the tug of his strokes at the ass now so near my face. I stand up and rub and slide my wet fingers into his now loosened hole. He groans with pleasure and so does the other. The top man slides the small jar of vas. to me, I grease him up and slowly bury my big hard prick into that warm furry butthole as it strokes and fucks away. We really move, this trio, and the room is now full of sucking and moaning. Finally they both come together and soon I follow.

Seconds after I come there is the sound of coins clinking to the floor and the tank top/middle man laugh-pants and says "Jackpot"... the onlookers and partakers grin ¿ laugh. Tom o' Finland in action.

Later Greg, who I've been stalking, reaches out at my first pass and soon his thick uncut prick is filling my throat right up. We trade on ¿ off and each give deep throat obsessive dives till I blast another killer into that gagging throat of his. What a great night – what a mess.

Later I tell Mark "I know I'm going to be 50 yrs old and be able to look back and say "I spent what I had to spend and used what was mine to use as it was intended." I loved it up.

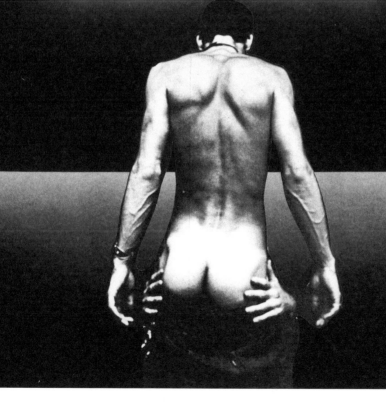

JUNE 26, '77 A red letter day. The Gay Rights parade, Christopher St. A day of total ecstasy & celebration with complete men & women. The faces that go with the images in these pages passed before me filled with the spirit of our basic need. My family from the Citoi had me Brazilian hips between the bubble machines and Robert & I beaming our beauty and love overflowing into the streets and finally to the source the sun the sun the sun & my arms & hands outstretched in communion & worship. The revelation of a martyr. Search the mere facts of his path to sainthood.

LIVING IN THIS BRAND NEW WORLD
MAY BE A FANTASY
BUT IT'S TAUGHT ME TO LOVE
AND THAT'S REAL
REAL
REAL TO ME.

JUNE 29, '77 Lesley Gore is quite a bore, but of course I get off on thinking of me connecting with her. That sense of "who'd have thunk it way back then…" I decide that I'm over my cold enough to do something about the sex energy that's been stored up. On a Wed. nite in a thick fog with explosions & sirens out on the street, the boys are into it in the back room. Joe and I cruise & connect and I melt him a bit. Reminds me of a blonde Peter. He's not very potent though & so I decline his invitation to spend the nite. We trade off a bit & then while he sucks me off I bend to the mustache with the damp crotch & quickly coax a snort of rush & a load of jizz out of him, then let it go for Joe. Much affection. On the street the cops checking out weird metallic fragments and "In the front room they're talking philosophy & in the back room they've got all the answers. You betcha." I miss Robert…

JUNE 30, '77 "Mind if I join you?" he said, but I couldn't hear him very well. "Do I have a joint?, No"… "Oh, no, sit down"
He says, "I saw you coming out of the bushes… does that mean you got what you wanted?" "I was just checkin' out the scenery," says I "Would you like to go inside again… I've got a nice cock… nice balls"…. He's so forthright I'm amused "Let's go & check it out" Those loose cotton drawstring pants show that he's not exaggerating. His big prick swells quickly at my touch and puts a juice spot on his pants. He loosens them and releases that warm sperm out & into my throat. He does me using his mouth and his big veined hands. We talk and discover mutual friends. City mouse country mouse. Frank, crazy Frank.

JULY 5, '77 Little Ceasar the gymnast, his occupation written all over his body. An emissary from the Isle of Dr. Moreau is this man, covered with soft blonde fur and with a bestial changeling quality in his face. We suck each other off on a table in the orgy room of the baths and I tell him "I want more but somewhere where its softer." He say, "How about your place?" He's a real surfer boy from New Jersey & accent & attitude and we roll and fumble for hours. He's up and off to the beach to get even redder. He say, "I'd like to get to know you better, but I'm leaving for LA in 3 days so what's the point." … I love it.

JULY 9, '77 That fucking ¼ moon drove me crazy tonight. Dancin' my tits right off with Robert at Alfies then drinkin come and sucking uncountable cocks 'til I'm hoarse & stained and thoroughly exhausted. Whew, that fucking moon… Crazy Mary wasn't kidding –

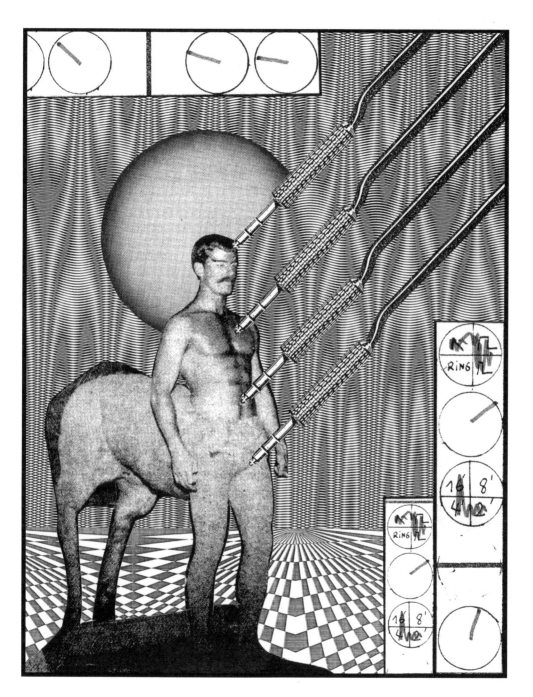

THE CITY

DISCO & ENTERTAINMENT | **MONTGOMERY AT BROADWAY**

JULY 10, '77 The night before the big party of '77 I see Valerie Carter, the yahooin' fool, finish up her week. Robt. ę I head on down, down to love town, we gonna take our bodies down to Alfies and disco up some love power. I am supercharged and the gods are movin' with me. I stop and connect with Frank Loverde (he's "holding up the wall") I am so full of love these days I'm overflowin' and Frank wants a taste. I say "what're you doing at the close of the nite?" He say, "Goin home." "You want some company?" "Yes"
Me Frank ę the puppy on the floor touching. Frank's beauty washes over me and through me and his body explores and fills and loves my body.
I am.

JULY 11, '77 Babies, what a night to remember. Tom Sanford throws a Save Our Human Rights Benefit at the City. Can I begin to try to enumerate the intense moments? Names – Eartha Kitt - Liz Torres – Charles Pierce – Martha Reeves – Sylvester, Jaye P. Morgan ę her tits, Izora Rhodes ę Martha Wash, Hodges, James ę Smith, Arthur Blake, *LADY BIANCA* – these were the focal points of the evening. The waves of intense energy … Primeval, tribal celebration the likes of which I've had such an unbelievable abundance of in my life. 7-11-77 and my life is blessed. God bless us all, Tiny Tim.

JULY 12, '77 Must be all that vitamin Q that Jake was talking about that's got me so buzzed up at 5 AM. Just met Henry at the tubs – we'd met under similar circumstances before ε I had taken him home ε tucked him in. What a sight, his big handsome body groovin' on my cock and eating me like dessert. Wanna show him off to a Jane Olivor crowd. Love him right up again, oh yes I can.

Talkin' with Martha Reeves in Tom's office after work. God I love that lady. I tell her its amazing the way she handled that mob of intensity. I tell her she's a strong woman. "Honey," she say, "with a crowd like that you do it all the way or you don't do it at all." She did it .

Ooh my baby loves me (He really really loves me)

Oh yeah (oh yeah!)

JULY 14, '77 - - Circles converging not a moment too soon - - Rusty's balls like two soft apricots hanging incredibly low from his uncut cock. I slide my tongue tip in between the shaft ε the foreskin and ride the rim. I give him the rhythm of swallowing muscles as I clamp my throat around his long prick and hold it there an incredibly long time. I had spotted him immediately and nodded hello as we've done before. But I knew it was time now. I watched ε followed and when it came time in the dance ("the lure of the dance") stuck my bulge in his face, which quickly pressed his warm lips to it. Hard-on slides past his fat sensual lips and deep into his mouth ε throat over ε over. I press my face into his slicked back hair ε feel the hollows of his cheeks with the backs of my hands as he sucks. I bend down into a crouch with him ε close to the floor we send our tongues where our cocks had just been. His protruding nipples ε moist asshole. . . . I turn him around ε he bends his hairy butt into my face, my long tongue diving madly into that soft soft hole as if the air I needed was in there. I slick his hole good with spit, stand up and slip my prick right in where he wants it. We move together, he gets it real deep and lovingly hard. I pace myself to the music.

Stravinsky ε Salsoul and, no shit, I blast the load right up his sweet ass and the music comes.

Janie knows how it feels . . . . she tells us about her adoration of singer Johnny Mathis and how the first time she saw him perform it was from the balcony next time last row orchestra, next first row and a week ago from backstage after opening his show to 5000 people. She says dream on and so do I. So do I. Rusty.

JULY 21, '77 S. Dorsky's house guests . . . . Steven from Seattle is so big – tall ɛ broad shouldered – suspenders and bearded and boyish and oh so sexy. After a big dinner I'm sitting with belt loosened. He comes up from behind and runs his hand across my hairy belly. He says let's spend the night together soon. Two days later he's my guest for M. Nightingale. He is a saving angel who dispels evil vibes with his mere presence.

We have a fabulous time fucking each other back and forth. I am so into his gorgeous butt I don't ever want to come. I hope Steven goes ahead and moves here ... I could make a habit of it ...

When *Reuben* walked into the dark room, I knew it was my time to finally meet him. He latches onto a partner and I gradually make my energy and intention felt through his shorts ɛ jock strap while he tirelessly works the guy over. I take him to my bed and his brown butt with a satyr's tail is a sight to behold as it curves away. "Work that butt hole" "Make your pee pee feel good" I love it. Next morning he lays me and we're off . . . .

AUG 23, '77 Sometimes you don't remember what it is that's missing till someone comes along and reminds you. *Light.*

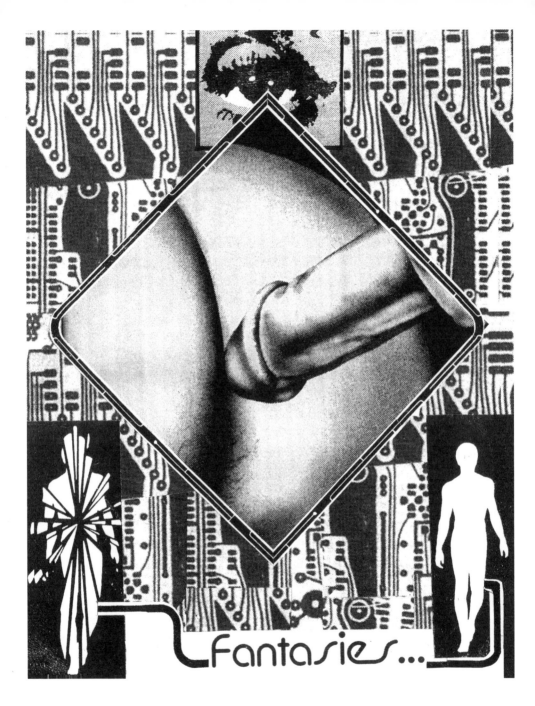

SEPT 1, '77 Back on the track. Romance is on the rise . . . Tonites menu a burger ȼ a fuck. The blond man bent over the table in the woodshed reminds me of fucking a tight woman . . . a great grip. I'm holding Gene in my heart though. We met in LA. Just two "good lookin, good natured" guys . . . There is nothing like a beautiful man staring into your eyes telling you what a beautiful man he sees. A circuit connects and the electrons rush along . . . . Absence lets the fantasies grow stronger. I want to reinforce the feeling and will fly back soon.

SEPT 25, '77 Well Dahling, no matter how you pretend you knew it would end this way. Charles Pierce concludes a five week run. *I Feel Love* rages on in the Disco (with me in the middle of it) Back to Africa.
Last night was divine with Artie on Potrero Hill. He's a special person Peter says. And a beautiful one. Powerfully built with an innocent expertise. Soft light colored fur covering pecs and his lovely furry ass full in my face. I give that Glory Thruway and Hallelujah . . hallelujah.

OCT 16, '77 Last week was a spoiler.

Everything comin my way –

The unique, incomparable Morgana King becomes my friend. She thinks I'm metaphysical . . . . Morgana, the Siren who sang to sailors from the rocks off the straits of *Messina* – "Don't come to my voice, follow my voice." Cocaine, champagne and joints ablaze in her Mark Hopkins suite – Come 5 AM we're still at it . . . she gives us stories of a life in the fast lane that touched upon Frank Sinatra, JFK, Marilyn, Joe DiMaggio, Billie Holiday, Al Pacino, Yogi Berra, Monty Rock III – a great singer for thirty years and a woman of earthy, real convictions. She will be an inspiration to me.

Meanwhile a sudden and even awesome stroke of good energy comes to me via the *MUSIC*. I wait for the next step with baited breath. What'll it be? A new turn in my life toward rewarded creativity? Casablanca Records possesses the extended, augmented version of "I Feel Love" and I await their judgment. Nevertheless an import-ant shift of perspective has taken place. I now realize my talents are valuable and are fast approaching a level of maturity sufficient to pay the rent. I'm ready for it. Ready to dive into the business of music and come up with my share of the larger life, The Extended, Augmented Version!

. . . .

I FEEL LOVE
Casablanca
Record and FilmWorks
EXTENDED VERSION
AUGMENTED VERSION

FEB 12, '78 *An evening with Morgana.*
Joints, talk, laugh, wonder around the suite suite with flan for the munchies ξ a Doris Day silent film.
The night before recording with Sylvester. Morgana asks me to put music to her "It Could Be Magic" – what a bloodline…
Chopin – Barry Manilow – Morgana King – Patrick Cowley
T.D. T.D.

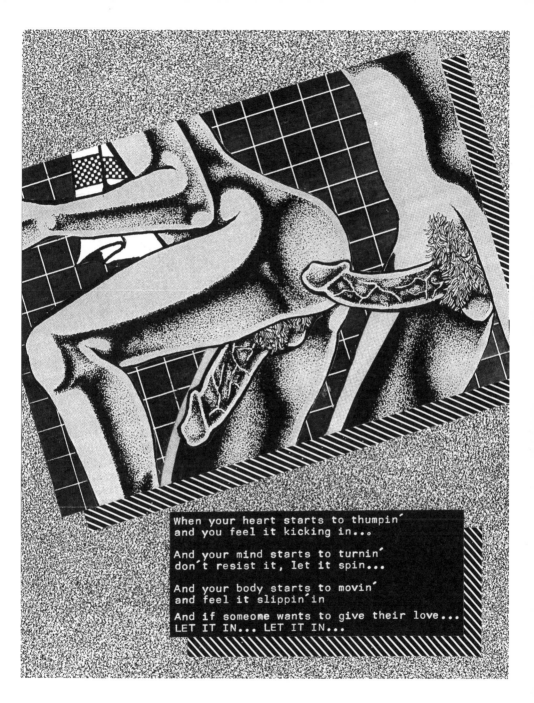

FEB 28, '78 Once in a leap year does a man like 668 come along. Not a thing could be improved except that he love me till his dying day. Futile to enumerate his dimensions, his hair, his skin, his direct gaze into my eyes as he stands over me and slides his uncut manhood in and into my ass, my grateful ass. Wordless enigmatic beguiling smile playing tentatively there – A single glancing pass at this flame and into the night air washed clean by warm spring rain … Singed and grateful for it.
When your heart starts to thumpin and you feel it kickin in…
And your mind starts to turnin don't resist it, let it spin…
And your body starts to movin and feel it slippin it
And if somebody wants to give their love … Let it in.. Let it in…

MAR 18, '78 On the way home from the studio where Jim Hicks ℰ I spaced out for hours, We spot a satyr baring his crack for us as he peers into store windows. He jumps a K ℰ I pursue. On Castro though he's too elusive for me ℰ I'm left horny ℰ hung up in front of the corner grocery. Just then Bobby comes bounding down the sidewalk ℰ flashes a big open hello to me, then rounds the corner. I think a minute, then make my move. We smoke a pipefull ℰ get acquainted. He's Soldier-of-the-Year back in Hawaii where he's stationed ℰ with much exuberance, passion ℰ non-citified energy he walks right into my heart (via my butt). He could eat me alive all night long.
Few days later, out in front of the Troc. we're in a quandary. Gary, Michael, Jim ℰ I can't get in w/out I.D. When up above me comes "Hey you sexy fucker." It's my solider-of-the-year; And knowing he's inside I approach the bouncer ℰ sweet talk our entry. When its time to go I start turning on to Bobby's old buddy Jim, Mr. California gymnast. We three get stoneder ℰ friendlier ℰ wind up rolling ℰ tumbling all night long in my bed. Me a slice of salami pressed warmly between these two loaves of French bread – Big boys each going at me ℰ each other… Jimmy spurts it all over his belly while Bobby bangs me from behind endlessly – I can take it till dawn from this baby boy – Soldier-of-the-year
————————————————————is my baby————————————————

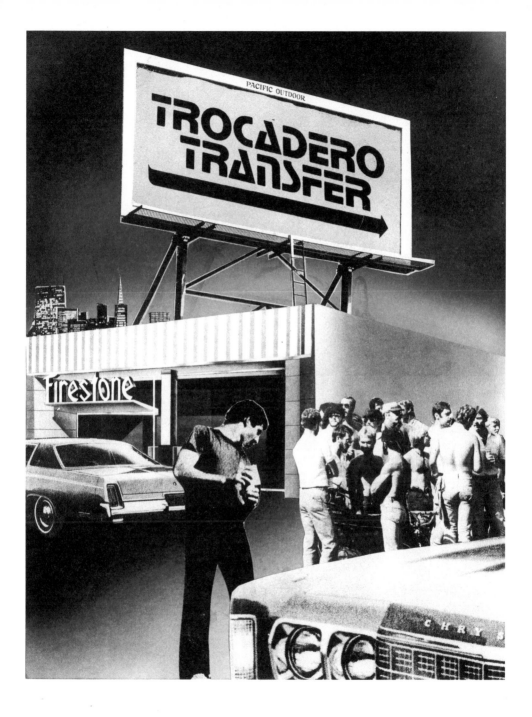

APR 10, '78 Patrick goes knocking on a door to garner info on a possible music project ¢ minutes later is banging away at a star baritone of the S.F. Opera – Woody T. and I and his 6'6" frame ¢ big ears –

APR 11, '78 At the tubs for maintenance I come across Warren. Love his lip and rub mine sore on his beard. Fuck his ample ass over ¢ over ¢ over ¢ again before I stumble home, info exchanged, see me next time you're here, Mendocino baby, and sing like you do to me all night long –

APR 13, '78 Jerry writes from Boston: "I fall in and out of affairs, bouncing from person to person like the ball in a pinball machine: bells ring, lights flash for a brief time and then I roll merrily on. Some become special, You are special
——————————————to me, friend"——————————————

APR 28, '78 Exercising my heterosexual prerogative or, Making love to Candice every 4 years or so... because of its rarity though it feels a bit heavy. Love her seam stockings ¢ high black boots stretched out in my bed. But my face gets lost in her pussy and the precise path to pleasure her is mysterious - ... Fun ...

APR 29, '78 Next night Byron comes in to see the Sluts. He's my new favorite buddy, with all the technotalk and common interests we have a good time together. I love banging his butt and his come audibly squirts into my hand.

APR 30, '78 Warren is expected tonite to see the show. I love getting over the hump and seeing someone for the second time – and from the entry a page ago I'll be enjoying his company very much – I love a man who knows how to kiss and can sing passion when he's being worked over –

MAY 24, '78 was a day to remember. Patrick opens the dream gig. *Sylvester & Loverde at the City.* High Energy crackling all around me – the sweat, the deep breath before Kickin in – the smell of a ton of fun across the stage – Sylvester's introduction … I have to tell you a story about Patrick, He used to shine the spotlight on us in our shows here but now its my pleasure to have the spotlight shine on him …
Frank & the girls looking & cookin fine down the line
Such a growing experience (as F. DANIS might put it) (I think he did say that to me, as a matter of fact) And at the end, grown as I was, came home to Sunni and an incredible sex scene – he licked me clean, a strand-o-cum looped round his muzzle! ho ho –
Thank you Jesus

Patrick J Cowley

Give me love with the music

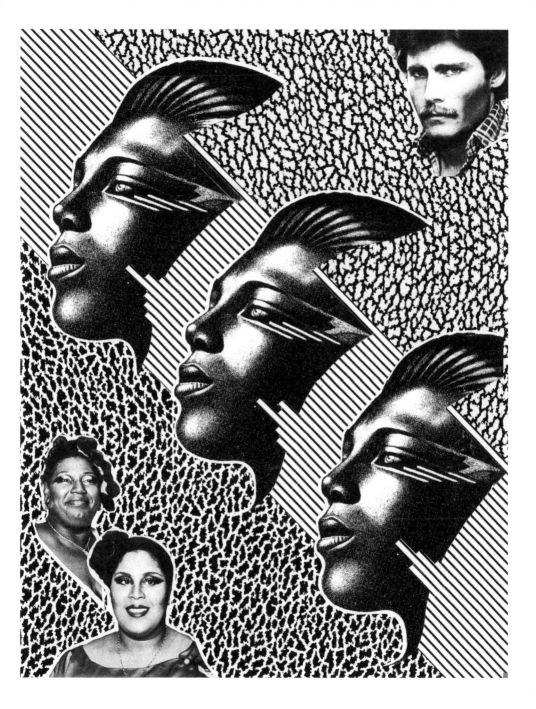

JAN 2, '79 Time to re-open? I'm not sure what I feel after months of ignoring these graphic accounts of one man's sex life. Does it cheapen to verbalize or more, to write about it – Do I care?

Seeing Tom now – we met only a couple of days after my return to SF from the Tour – The Tour – well, first there was Paul ¿ I rooming together, sleeping together, eating together, on the bus on the beach – couldn't help but be a bit intense after a few weeks – He departs, I lighten up.

In Wash. I meet George, the bartender from the "Eagle" – he'd love a load of piss but the plumbing won't cooperate. Our cards get switched ¿ I take a plastic piece of his identity with me – In Chicago, at sound check, Kerry makes like the party boy ¿ turns us on to dope – later we meet at "Man's Country" and fuck and suck for hours – moving on to a roomful later with Robert, his friend George ¿ a bearded *"Boromir"* – those Chicago boys throw a good party – In Houston I see *MARION* again – my beautiful friend. In New York I meet Kerry again at the St. Marks ¿ it's phase two, in which Doris gets her oats. Also met John Vaught – my steward Italiano –

On to Frankfurt and the little Folsom St. bar *"Boots"* on a frigid Monday nite – while putting the make on my German student friend whose name has vanished I'm thrust upon by an overzealous patron in suspenders who finds it hard to understand "no". Later in my student friend's apt. I devour his Christmas cookies from Mom ¿ stroke his strange long body – then gone – London – London

In London I meet first Carlos, the handsome bartender at the Napoleon club. So fine ¿ dark – from *MALTA*. We make a date for later in the week. Next nite out at the Embassy disco I see John K. down below dancing freely – I like his moves ¿ his strange tattered shirts – I look again ¿ he's dancing alone – I join him ¿ we hit it off – Later, in the cold wet London winter we're illegally zooming across Londontown on his motorcycle. That nite, at one point John is changing the music, bent over the records I grease his ass with the honey from the tea tray ¿ sweet fuck him standing up – later for me too – with that strange warm sensation from honey in my ass – We spend our two days together – There's John seeing to it that I'm on the correct bus to take me back to my hotel – a small wave of his hand – we're apart – Paris, Rome & home to my boys – And they're everywhere & beautiful to see in cafés, on the street, the shops, the busses – To concentrate on other things takes work – So work, child & make these prophecies come true – Success is in the stars says the voice over the phone – Positive energy … positive energy

MAY 17, '80 Angels of Lights ... Holy Cow Show – White Trash Boom Boom... Nothing is Sacred Show ... Up above the packed auditorium next to Sandy & PAOLI – A long seduction ... conversational inclusions ... lingering legs and warm arms brush & connect filling me with sexual energy ... He's committed to another so I must take it to the street – Jaguar – sucking that big bearded dick that moans and hisses oh yeah I slam his big ass while he begs me to give him what he deserves he needs he gets but turn around and I am gone –
Burn Brighter Flame
Burn Brighter Flame
Burn till the world refuses
love to none ...

MAY 18, '80 The ridiculous neon brown and pink flesh tanned around the middle slick lips and hand unrelenting rush and crowd me out of my bed.

JUNE 5, '80 At Richard B's birthday gathering I fall into Rick's dark brown eyes & dark brows Black Irish. At home after the party, I call back & make a movie date for the next day.

OCT 10, '80 Standing near the blonde ȼ bearded Norseman as he works a man over. I've watched him coast to coast ȼ I've waited for my moment. Tonight I stuff his fat *prick* down my throat 'til his metal cock ring rests under my teeth. Stroking soft hair ȼ nuzzling my face into his beard ȼ chest he moans he swallows my stiff cock His come on my lips My jizz creams into his waiting mouth His furry thighs … "I just did" …

OCT 19, '80 The big-three-o – I wonder to myself if many people can burst into momentary tears at the wave of happiness that breaks over me – the realization that my life, body, music is so beautiful. Working like a possessed man this past week – Ice Age, Paradise, X-time, Thief of Love, Make it Come Loose, Hold On …
Last night, birthday eve, after days of *Porno-phonics,* I scurry to the bookstore ȼ pick up Lee, with the cast on the finger ȼ hand his lover broke for him. The moon slipping into the fog above the hill. The red tower rising science-fiction. Lee's deep throat, I grease his ass and, upside down I ease my dick into his warm hole ȼ he moans my name as the porno-phonic raves on. Afterwards we lay endlessly my soft dick still buried inside him. I sing Yea Yea Yea …

1974-1976

CHARGOYLE

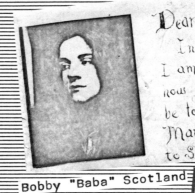

Jorge "Georgie" Socarrás

Bobby "Baba" Scotland

Pat n´ Theresa McGinley

Pat n´ Jorge Baca

Bobby "Baba" Scotland

Diamond Sunday

Janice "Baby" Sukatis

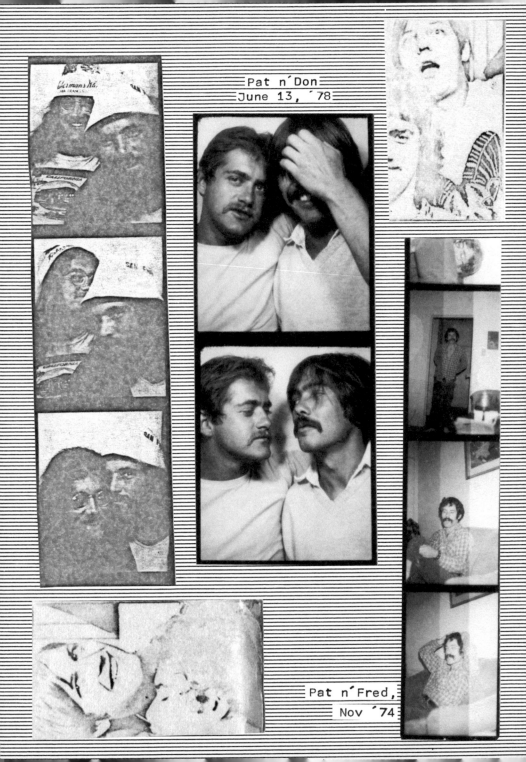

Pat n´Don
June 13, ´78

Pat n´Fred,
Nov ´74

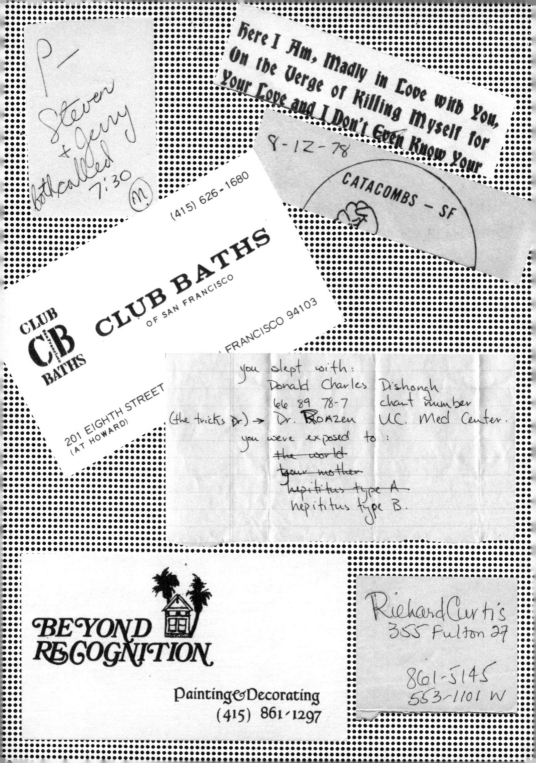

SYLVESTER returns to The City Wednesday through next Sunday with his new show. Performances are at 9 and 11 p.m.

THE CARBON
ALTERNATIVE
THANK YOU

03-20-78

3 Tx $1.40
          $1.40 TxSt
          $0.09 Tx
          $1.49 Co TL

00-057 No E

Dear Patrick,

as you may have noted - telephone conversation is not exactly my forte - hopefully I can do better on paper.

I have made several suggestions regarding being together - to explore ideas of possible mutual interest. They are there, but we are just not sharing the same space at this time.

As it stands - the bottom line is a) I like to ball with you and b) I like to listen to your music.

As I dislike standing around in bars & would prefer several steady fucks

please give a call when you'd like a no-hassle piece of ass - or an appreciate audience for your music

Pat Reed

Jim Meeks
4034 20Th
621-5296

drawing by
Francesca Rosa

Suzanne "Pickles" Thompson

Bobby "Baba" Scotland